Survival Was Only The Beginning

A Costa Concordia Story

Cover design by Blitzprint Inc.

Cover photograph by: Giuseppe Modesti

ISBN # 978-0-9919790-0-4

Survival Was Only the Beginning

A Costa Concordia Story

Author Contact Information:

www.andreadaviscostaconcordia.com

andreadaviscostaconcordia@gmail.com

II Edition

Andrea Davis is a member of the Canadian Association of Professional Speakers.

A percentage of the proceeds of the sale of this book will be donated to the Carlo Piscane School on the island of Giglio. Laurence and Andrea Davis would like to honor and thank the locals for their dedication to the safety of the survivors of the Costa Concordia and their contribution to environmental education and reestablishment of the natural resources of Giglio.

To Cory

Sail away with us
on this incredible
journey —

Andrea Davis

ACKNOWLEDGMENTS

This is a memoir. The events described in this book truly happened. The people most responsible for this book are the crew of the *Costa Concordia*, co-passengers, islanders of Giglio, locals of Porto Santo Stefano and staff at the Canadian Embassy in Rome, my entire family and so many friends who have trusted me to tell this story faithfully. In the course of my writing, I contacted almost everybody mentioned plus many others. It would be impossible for me to list everyone, so I will not even try.

I am deeply grateful for the time and support offered so generously by my family and friends. My profound thanks go to so many that I hardly know where to start.

I'd like to say thanks to my dear husband Laurence for the countless hours on end, days and nights that I have been at my computer, compiling this memoir. Your support and encouragement has been invaluable and my drive to continue when I have not known where the next chapter was going to lead to. We have been blessed to travel this journey together. We will continue to share the rewards of this book together, as we hear of readers' fascination, comments, criticism and delight.

Thank you Laurence, you are truly my *Lionheart*!

I sincerely want to thank Bob Bannon, my book mentor and friend. Without you Bob, this project would not have been possible. You have been my inspiration, my motivation, encouragement and support. You have believed in me; you have been my driving force.

Thanks too, to Leanne Bannon who has helped in the finishing touches of this book. Together you have helped to make this possible. Thanks to various editors and graphic designers who have assisted in the completion of this book.

I have tried to recreate events, locales and conversations from my memories. In doing so, I regret if I have omitted anybody that I have met along the way, misspelled names or places or misquoted events or dates.

Although I have made every effort to ensure that the information in this book was correct at press time, I do not assume and hereby disclaim any liability to any party for errors or omissions resulting from negligence, misinformation, information that might have been forgotten due to the nature of this trauma, or any other cause.

For Laurence

My Lionheart

Prologue

Writing this book has allowed me to explore the many levels of what I have been going through. I have endeavored to communicate my emotions, actions, fears and the glory of survival as clearly as possible. So much has happened since our story began on Friday, January 13, 2012, and as time dilutes our memories, we feel in danger of forgetting the important moments.

The reality is that living through and after a life-altering disaster changed everything we thought we knew about ourselves and our connection to God. We could never recover if we remained in a state of shock and turmoil; trying to remember everything, process the emotions, and accept the grief, while moving forward with our daily activities. Thus, in writing this memoir, I have allowed my experience to reach the core of my soul and I am grateful for the gift of this emotional exposure. I have been granted the ability to share my life with loved ones, both today and in years and generations to come.

For our Grandchildren: Caleb, Jaron, Judah and Kiley, and those who may follow.

We present this chronicle as a legacy - that we were saved for some higher purpose. We thank God that our lives were spared and we returned home to our family. We are blessed with the opportunity to spend many more years together with you, our precious offspring. We cherish our ability to watch you grow, to see your expressions as you listen to our account, reminding you of our adventure on the historic *Costa Concordia.*

One day we will sound to you the same as when Great Grandpa would relate his war-time stories as we all listened in awe.

Like our ancestors, we too are survivors.

Survival was only the beginning.

You brought us home.

CONTENTS

CHAPTER 1

Bang, Crash… Boom

We were finally seated in the elegant Milano Restaurant, the focal point of this world-class cruise ship, the *Costa Concordia*. The room reflected itself through the large glass expanse, the only light outside the windows was from the moon and stars shimmering above the open waters of the Mediterranean.

Unable to pull ourselves away from the ambience of the Atrium and the toe-tapping rhythm of Jazz and Blues, we arrived late to dinner. It was 9:30 p.m. on Friday, January 13, 2012. We entered the Milano dining room and were seated with Tata and Mike as we had been over the previous few nights. All around us was laughter and new friends enjoying a shared meal. Against all cruise ship rules, we had smuggled a bottle of Rum Chata Cream Liqueur into the dining room. We congratulated ourselves as we sampled our contraband.

Jokes and stories punctuated the relaxed conversation as we anticipated the culinary delight being placed in front of us. The mouth-watering smell of gourmet food, shoes kicked off under the table, servers bustling about the late night diners, dishes and cutlery clinking as waiters worked around nearby tables, a sip of red wine – something not right.

We jumped from friendly chaos to outright panic in the blink of an eye. What was it? What did I hear? I looked at Laurence, his eyes wide. I could see in his vague look of disbelief that he felt it too. There was a brief moment of uncertainty, of confusion, of question. A single moment of dread before ...

Crash, crunch, scraping noises, then complete darkness.

Immediately, the ship listed, cracking and grating. We went from sitting on a level surface to spilling over at a crazy angle. We could barely stand up straight. My clothes were soaked in red wine and hot food.

Screaming and crying. Glasses and bottles tumbling. Dishes shattering. Drinks and food everywhere.

We ducked beneath our table, trying to protect ourselves from the falling daggers of glass and shards of wood. Panic surrounded us.

"Laurence, grab my purse and shoes from under the table."

The emergency generators came on and a low light filled the room. At last, we could see the chaos all around us.

"Attention, attention. We are experiencing an electrical problem that is currently being taken care of. Please remain calm; we will keep you updated."

The announcement came in multiple languages, English last. It was difficult to hear instruction over panicked passengers and frenzied, injured staff. We scrambled to our knees, crawling along the floor trying to avoid the falling glass, chandeliers, plates, food, and drink. I heard Tata's panicked voice as she shouted across amplified noises to Mike, "I will not get back on board tomorrow after port. I would rather fly home."

We did not know that no one would get back on board. But first we had to get off.

We scrambled out of the dining room, stampeding behind thousands of frantic people. We abandoned the smells of the meal and exotic beverages and squeezed through the narrow doorways. We were met with mass commotion.

People pushed and ran in every direction.
Time seemed endless.
Panic amplified the fear and confusion.
Hysteria and pandemonium in all directions.
And no information.

"I'm going to our cabin to get our life jackets," Laurence called out to me.

"Don't leave me; we will never find each other."

It was this, my need to not lose him in the crowd, which ultimately became our lifesaver.

We tried to get to our room but the elevators no longer worked. We realized that with the power out, even if we could reach our room, our key cards were useless. Without them, the door that closed behind us a mere two hours earlier now sealed in everything we had with us.

Together, in this state of confusion, we made our way back to the frenzy in the Atrium on deck three, where we were entertained only a short while before, feeling safer and somewhat comforted being close to the Guest Services desk. We hovered behind a family holding on to their elderly mother's wheelchair. The brakes were on, restraining the chair from sliding down and crashing into whatever was in the way.

"This is a sensible place to wait for instruction," I screamed to Laurence.

I expected the Guest Services staff would be the first to hear instruction and would be able to relay information and answer our concerns. If we remained with this family, there was a better chance we would have a clear and guided path if there was an evacuation, being behind the elderly, disabled woman. Weren't the elderly, the children, and the infirm supposed to be rescued first? Not knowing what to think, so much going through our minds. Was this the first sign of the survival instinct beginning to take hold?

The crew would know what to do.

We watched the Guest Relations staff tape computer monitors to the desk and lavish floral arrangements in glass vases to the counter tops as everything continued to slide.

The list of the ship rapidly increased.

I recall the smile of the young lady behind the desk. She was trained to smile, no matter what.

We could not hear or understand their words, but we could see the confusion in the crew as they mumbled amongst themselves.

Time seemed to stop as minutes felt like hours.

Beep, beep, beep ... seven short beeps followed by a long signal.

"Attention, attention, all passengers make your way to deck four to abandon ship." Once again, English was the last in the list of languages as we awaited our turn to understand the instructions.

Tumult, commotion, and panic everywhere.

There was no space on the congested staircase so we tried to wait our turn.

Pushing and shoving, we made our way up as fast as we possibly could. We were on the stairs, one level higher than the seeping water.

Water gushed through the doors and down the hallways. The Mediterranean Sea spread everywhere.

Where to now? Out to the crowded deck? Portside? Starboard? Where was our muster station?

We edged our way onto the Portside of the deck following the crowds, not knowing which direction we were facing or where our muster station was.

Among the deluge of people ahead of us, there was no space for us. Wherever there was a gap, an opening in the thousands of panic stricken people, we pushed forward. The survival instinct was beginning to move into a higher gear now. The list of the ship was becoming too steep for the lifeboats to reach the water at this angle. Passengers who had thought they were being saved and had made their way onto lifeboats, were instructed back onto the sinking ship as the lifeboats could not be lowered to the water below. On deck, we were told to cross over the hallways to get to the Starboard deck.

At last, we reached Starboard, deck four - cold, fresh air, the smell of the sea, and fear. This was the deck where we were supposed to be. We were told to come here to evacuate. This is where the lifeboats would be waiting. But this was not a place of hope. We fought against gravity. Objects were flying, people scrambling, bodies falling like ten-pins, bones breaking, doors off hinges, faces through glass panes, blood everywhere.

Children cried, mothers screamed, sons and fathers helped the disabled and injured, the babies and the young.

Crowds were everywhere, space a forgotten luxury. Where were we all heading?

There seemed to be no escape. Most passengers found life vests, but we were not able to go back to our cabin. "There will always be life vests at your muster station" we were told at the emergency drill on the first day of our voyage.

But where was our muster station?

No instructions, no directions, just a stampede of hysteria.

Screaming, crying, panic, and chaos reigned around us. Reaching the gate to the lifeboat ahead, we heard them call, "Place for one more only." I signaled to the person behind us to take the lone spot.

We made our way to the next life boat. Eventually one life jacket was thrown out of a lifeboat that had no more place for passengers. Laurence put this on, knowing he would do whatever possible to be my savior. He feared for my ability to cope if we were forced into the water; my arthritic knees and recent hip replacement would make swimming difficult. Laurence's nature was to take charge and to protect me.

It felt like an eternity until I too, was able to retrieve a trampled life jacket from the floor of the crowded deck. Desperate for support and guidance, an elderly lady who spoke no English, joined us. We were now three.

We created space for our dependent by forming a human chain. Laurence and I switched sides so he could use his stronger, dominant left arm. This left me to use my frail and exhausted right as we clung to the railings. We had to hold ourselves up; the ship was so slanted we could no longer stand straight. We were thrust from pillar to post, trying to get the three of us to the front. We were squished between the crowds of desperate people; trying everything to reach a life boat, our only hope.

How much longer would it take to ready enough lifeboats to evacuate everyone?

The mass of metal was churning, thrusting, listing, and tumbling under and over us. How much longer would we be able to hang on? How much longer would the ship remain afloat?

When we reached the front rail, I looked out at the sea. An almost full moon projected a divine light across the water. I could see lights blinking in the distance and had an overwhelming feeling of relief; we could possibly be close to land. I had no idea how far we really were, distances become so distorted in the dark. Our bodies were bashed and bruised from our journey. As the ship rolled beneath us, we crashed into steel posts, rails, doors, and people.

We were two who had become three. The elderly lady had been standing alone and was so afraid, we had to help her. Together we were filled with disappointment each time we got to a lifeboat that was full. But we were also afraid of getting onto the overcrowded lifeboats. .

People were jumping from the upper decks, landing on top of others in lifeboats below. The crew was confused. With a lack of knowledge and faulty equipment, they were struggling to launch the lifeboats. As the angle of the sinking vessel increased, it restricted their release. The lifeboats were crashing and slamming against the side of the ship. Some were dropping and fell meters before hitting the water below. People's screams of fear were followed by those of relief, as some boats left the side of the ship. They sailed away into the darkness of the night, but to where? Would they come back for us?

"Don't leave me," I said to Laurence, over and over.

Laurence was desperately asking for help. Where must we go, what must we do? What was the announcement? We missed it. We could neither hear nor understand anything.

"On behalf of the Captain…."

Was the Captain going to make an announcement that we would all be comforted by or that explained the circumstance and the strategy to abandon ship? The bellowing of the tumbling ship, the cries all around us blocked out all other sounds. We were surrounded by the desperate sound of panic and fear.

"They don't understand you and can't answer you. They don't know any more than we do," I tried to explain to Laurence in my attempt to help keep him calm. I felt possessed by a sense of serene tranquility.

I was so used to being in control. But on this night, control was taken from me; how were we going to cope?

People were screaming, bodies flying, and the ship was slowly sinking. We grasped the railing to keep from falling, or slipping and sliding into the black waves. There were still no instructions, no assistance, and no helping hands. Were we supposed to jump or would we simply crash and sink into the inky oblivion?

I kept having visions of the movie "Titanic" and asked Laurence to sing to me. He was lost for words. I watched him and thought how beautiful he was, although not as handsome as Leonardo DiCaprio. I giggled to myself. I always teased that he couldn't sing, but tonight I wished he would in a gentle voice.

"Sing to me," I cried. I wanted his words to drown out everything I was hearing.

I pictured the scene of DiCaprio's serenade as the Titanic sank.

Was this going to be our fate too? Laurence had hope but I was afraid. I realized the ship was going down, that we were sinking. I refused to think about death. Emotionally I was numb; I did not fear death. I was afraid of the unknown and the potential suffering - we had no idea, second by second of where we would be in a moment's time. The pain on Laurence's face and the expression of horrified confusion was my immediate despair. We thought of our family back home, our children and grandchildren.

“We have life insurance,” Laurence reassured me.

Laurence told me after our rescue, how he had thoughts of the security that we had provided for our family. We felt so blessed we had financially made provision for their future. At the time, this was emotionally comforting.

My fear was immediate; my thoughts were moment to moment. I focused only on my next move, putting one foot forward at a time.

It was up to us.

People continued jumping on top of those already in the few remaining rescue boats. The ship was now listing beyond where we could hold ourselves up. There was still no lifeboat; never enough room for the three of us.

We moved down the deck, clutching the railing – clutching on to life. We kept moving forward in search of new hope, another lifeboat.

Overwhelmed and panic stricken crew members were shouting in confusion and some people from the other rescue vessels were tugging and pulling on a faulty mechanism. It was supposed to eject the barrel, the inflatable rescue vessel that was meant to glide out of the capsule once released and lowered. *Rip, thud, splash.*

The barrel had disengaged and dropped to the sea, the shell cracked, and the life boat began inflating. Was this our last remaining hope for escape?

But was it too late? The ship was sinking faster and rescue efforts were frenzied. Our hopes were becoming trapped under the beams of the *Costa Concordia*; our only remaining rescue vessel was quickly deflating.

The ship was sinking beneath our feet as the sea was rising.

The Coast Guard and emergency vessels were far out of reach. We fought the instinct to give in to panic. Realization dawned, one second, two… The water was closer. At my feet, my shoes, my pants, my soul - everything was getting wet.

There was no longer a choice to be made. We had too much to live for. We looked at the forlorn lady, the lady who had reached out to us with all her trust.

We had to let her go. We released our grip and as we left her behind. I prayed for her safety.

Laurence and I looked at each other. At this moment we had only each other. Would we remain together or must we kiss and say goodbye? Desperately holding onto each other, we tried to have faith and move in the direction of our destiny, whatever that would be.

No longer could we wait to try and understand another language. No longer could we wait to listen for what was not being said. We could no longer wait to be told what we must do.

There was no other way out; swim towards the distant lights or sink with the ship.

How fortunate we were that both of us could swim. We could not think of the alternative.

Following my recent hip replacement I had taken to swimming three to four times a week. Swimming had become a way of life for me. I had no way of knowing that my investment in aqua fitness would prepare me for this fateful swim. Laurence and I had no one but each other to depend on. We were now in control. Together, holding onto each other, we had to take charge.

The water before us was clearly visible thanks to the bright moon. We looked toward the flickering lights on the other side of the sea, looked at each other. God help us…

Splash…

At 12:10 a.m., almost three hours after we sat down to dinner, Laurence's watch stopped working as he hit the water.

CHAPTER 2

Then It Shall Be... the Costa Concordia

Laurence would turn 60 on December 30, 2011. "Let's celebrate by cruising the Mediterranean on our way home from South Africa," I had suggested with a smile.

On December 25, 2011, we left home to visit family in Johannesburg and Cape Town. We were introduced to our beautiful, new granddaughter Kiley and visited our son, my 83-year-old mother, aunts, sister, nieces, nephews, and friends.

We had such a great time traveling down memory lane and enjoying precious moments together. Since immigrating to Canada in 1997, our return trips to South Africa always ended in emotional ripples, love, and ultimately, separation. One more visit, one more farewell. We had thought that this trip would end on a more positive note.

For years we had dreamed of sailing across the Mediterranean. I spent many hours researching, planning, reading reviews, letters, and reports. Two days in Barcelona followed by our eighth cruise. The dates worked out perfectly and the route sounded so exciting.

Costa was new to us as our previous voyages had been on American-based cruise liners, sailing out of the USA, Canada and Caribbean ports.

We had become cruise junkies over the last few years and could think of no better way than onboard a ship to see, travel, eat, laugh, learn, and have fun. We never needed an excuse to go on a cruise; it was our favorite way to spend our down time.

I had traveled through Europe in the late 70's during my footloose and fancy-free youth. This was Laurence's first trip to Europe and he loved every moment. It was so exciting for me to share in the enthusiasm of my husband's first European adventure. The early days on board and the land-based explorations and tours are moments that we will remember forever.

We left Barcelona on Monday, January 9, 2012, sailing on the *Costa Concordia*. We were just two of the 4,200 people on board - approximately one thousand crew members and 3,200 passengers. We were from around the world - nearly one thousand Italians, hundreds of French, British, Russians, Germans, and even a few from Argentina, Peru, Canada, South Africa, and Israel. Our friend Tata was from Norway and many more from the USA and India.

The ship was just about twice the size of The Titanic and compared in size to the length of 3 soccer fields. She boasted 17 decks, a floating pleasure palace. There were 1,500 luxury cabins, 6 restaurants, 13 bars, the two-story Samsara Spa and Fitness Center, the three-story Athene Theatre, 4 swimming pools, the Barcelona Casino, the Lisbona Disco, and even an Internet Café.

1: LAURENCE AND ME ON BOARD THE COSTA CONCORDIA

Palma De Mallorca, Spain; Cagliari, Sardinia; Palermo, Sicily; Civitavecchia, Rome, Italy; Savona, Italy; Marseille, France; and back to Barcelona – this was our planned itinerary. We had been dreaming of the Mediterranean for years and it was finally here.

Our daily activities are always so adventurous and exciting. As much as we love being on the ship while cruising, we also love the anticipation of arriving at each port. As we sail into each port, Laurence and I love being on our balcony with my camera and Laurence's binoculars. The nature and the architecture is enthralling and as we get closer and closer, we appreciate seeing the people and hearing new languages being spoken by the people on shore. Yet another destination to mark off on our travel map. Although we only spend a few hours in each new country, this allows us time to explore and to mingle with the locals. Some days, we join cruise excursions in order to maximize all there is to see and to do in a short period of time. In other ports, Laurence and I enjoy taking a taxi or getting onto a local bus. We walk miles and miles, in sunshine or in rain. We love mingling with locals over lunch, coffee or a glass of wine. We visit churches, synagogues, museums and landmarks. Some days we are so happy, just being together on a beach or in a park simply, people watching.

The history and culture of people in each new city is so exciting for us both. We love shopping and eating ice cream as we make our way back to port. Day by day, another beautiful adventure - always to be followed by the glorious sight of the ship in front of us as we return to the port, once again to sail off to our next destination. We love the glory and pride as each day we walk up the gangway to be greeted by the crew. "Welcome back, Mr. and Mrs. Davis. Have you had a nice day?" Our passenger cards are swiped through security as we hear the signal "ting, ting". A beautiful feeling of security, identity and belonging, followed by the exciting anticipation of sailing out to sea. Relaxation and entertainment await us.

Friday, January 13, 2012, day four of a seven-day route. We had an amazing day roaming the streets in Rome: Saint Peters Square, the Coliseum, the ancient

Synagogue, pizza on the sidewalk for lunch, followed by a visit to the Spanish Steps, Trevi Fountain, and a marathon. Back to the Hop-On Hop-Off bus, back to meet our tour group and return to the majestic *Costa Concordia.* We would return in time to sail from Civitavecchia, 40 miles northwest of Rome, to Genoa, our next port of call.

2: Our amazing day in Rome

After the most exhilarating day in Rome, our friends, Mike and Tata whom we'd met on the second day, were waiting for us at the excursion bus, arms laden with Louis Vuitton, Burberry, and other bags displaying their pleasure over the riches of Rome. We rode back sharing our euphoria and excitement and boarded the ship in Civitavecchia excited about the next leg of the journey.

Hundreds of new passengers also lined up to board; it was to be their first night at sea. Excitement was in the air as they anticipated their magnificent week ahead. Their itinerary was Rome to Rome in seven days. They seemed as excited as we were; the day they had dreamed of was here.

We met Mike and Tata for drinks in the glamorous Atrium of the *Costa Concordia*. Tonight's feature was the music of New Orleans. We were swept away.

Fingers snapping, toes tapping, we listened to one of the passengers, an incredible jazz vocalist, perform with the resident pianist. People dressed in elegant evening wear crowded around, leaning over the 11 levels of railings looking down into the courtyard, enraptured by the rhythms.

We were overjoyed when we pulled ourselves away from the music, already late for dinner.

Chapter 3

The Silence of the Freezing Mediterranean

Dark, cold, and mechanical; I kicked off my shoes. We must swim. The moon seemed to be getting closer, the ship farther as she receded from where we left her.

"Laurence, don't leave me!"

He flipped onto his back and we tried to calculate how far we were from the tumbling mess that was once the *Costa Concordia*, and how far we were from the shore. We heard others jumping in behind us. Swim, we could not think of the consequences, we could not think of the risk. My God, it was freezing cold.

"Don't leave me," I shouted as Laurence held on to my life jacket with one hand.

"Kick, swim," I heard as we stroked our way farther from the crashing roars of the dying ship.

"Don't leave me…"

How much farther until we get to soft sand?

"Are there sharks in the sea?" I shouted.

The Mediterranean sunshine was a distant dream; the night had become a horror.

Freezing cold, frozen limbs – kick splash, our past, our future – we must get home.

The huge yellow chimney was keeling over and roaring as it fell faster. We must swim and get out of its way.

We had cleared the falling tower.

We had beaten her. She was still tumbling, but we were out of her reach. We were going to make it to land. But how much further did we have to go?

"Swim, kick, swim," Laurence repeated to me between rhythmic strokes.

I remembered my recent hip replacement and started coaching myself. Don't let go. With all my strength I was willing it on; it must not slip, it must not snap.

"Don't leave me," I screamed to Laurence again.

People were splashing behind me. I could do it, I could lead the way.

Was this the reason I had taken up Aqua Aerobics in recent months? Was this the reason lap swimming had become something I loved rather than the chore of an exercise routine? I was scared, numb with cold and feeling a mixture of relief and fear.

Chapter 4

The Journey of Survival

The blinking lights were getting closer and the stranded screams farther away; we had to be nearing the shore and soft, warm beach sand.

But instead of welcoming, easy to ascend beaches, we were met with cold, high, towering rocks and nothing to grab onto.

Reach. Climb. Nothing to put my feet on. Nowhere to step.

Slide. Scrape. Reach.

Cold. Slimy.

Grating noises. Rough. Rugged. Sharp.

Pushing behind me, pulling ahead of me. I must do it. I had come too far to be beaten by rock.

The rocks were cold and tall. Animal instinct and the will to survive overtook fear and cold. We reached the top, freezing and frightened. (Laurence now calls me Spiderman.)

The dark was filled with screams and frenzy.

I was wet and cold, freezing and fearful. The salty water burned as it dripped into my eyes. It ran down my back leaving me frozen. Had we survived all of this only to succumb to the cold?

By the light of the moon, I could see the tears of cold and fear leaking down Laurence's cheeks as he stood shaking, shivering and crying. There was nowhere to go.

"I need to pee," he whispered between his quivering lips.

"You're wet already," I said.

His pee was warm, trickling down his legs settling between the thread of his frozen salt-caked jeans.

The animal in us let go of all else but the will to survive.

How long would we be waiting? Was the tide coming over the rocks to pull us back to the ship? How much time did we have?

Who were these other people that followed us once we leaped into the sea? What did they go through to reach this solid land? Were we going to survive? Together was our only hope.

Voices calling out and screaming for partners and friends. It was pitch dark. Nobody could see who had gotten across and climbed the steep rock. Nobody could see who had succumbed to the freezing cold water, who had given up the strength to get to the other side or who had been picked up by returning lifeboats. Tears and saltwater burned our eyes, darkness magnified our desolation.

Huddled together, we grasped and cuddled, we cried and shivered. We were no longer just two. With a group we had a better chance of staying warm and of being found. Human contact and comfort was our only common language. We had all found hope, if not safety. We had to pray – together.

In the distance we could see flashing lights; we could hear the sirens and the motors roaring. We saw and heard helicopter rotors whizzing and hovering over the sea, the light beams in the opposite direction. Their focus was on the ship.

We were stranded.

I sat down on a rock; I could no longer stand. In front of my eyes I gazed and watched as the *Costa Concordia* sank, taking with her everything that we had traveled with. Our favorite jewels, our money and passports, our phones, cameras and computers. Our favorite clothes and possessions and all the gifts and souvenirs that we had been given and bought on this remarkable trip.

Together, we watched her go down.

Lights on the ship flickered off. Life grew quiet. We began to feel totally exhausted and weak. We stared into sullen emptiness.

Did anybody notice that we had climbed the rocks? That we scaled above the sea, and she was coming back? How much time did we have? We could hear the tide rising.

Icy, frozen, piercing cold enveloped us until we could feel nothing else.

Shivering and crying.

Tears of fear, of pain, of hope.

Brutal, frigid, wet.

Screams and tears in languages we could not understand, but didn't need to. This was universal. Terror and despair filled us all.

The rocks were wet beneath my feet, the tide smashing into the surface of the cliff.

The circle of man, the comfort of other bodies…

Was I hearing voices in the distance? I was seeing the light beams from cell phones as locals were searching for stranded passengers.

People had seen the blinking lights of our life jackets from afar and called the local Police.

Was this real? Were we being saved? Was I really seeing people coming from the other side of the rocks?

I called him "Buddy". He was in front of me leading the way.

Buddy was working on the Concordia at the time of this disaster. It was probable that he had worked a 16 hour shift leading up to the moment of this accident. Buddy's life, his security, and his future were shattered like the ship.

My frozen hands were clutching the back of his pants. His uniform was his pride; his belt was my strength. It was holding me up.

My feet - cold, pain, crack and crunch. Left, right, I can do it. We were directed away from the water. I must follow. Buddy, lead the way.

Laurence was behind me, "Don't leave me, don't let go."

He ripped the blinking light off his life jacket and bent down to light a path for me to walk. I could not see. I could not feel. I could barely hear. Cold, freezing, and pain.

"Oh my God, look at your feet…." Without my shoes, the rocks had shredded my feet. But they were too cold for me to notice.

"How much do you weigh?" Buddy asked. "Get onto my shoulders," he demanded.

Buddy was half my size but had twice my spirit.

"Twice as much as you do Buddy. I will walk. We are all in this together," I said. "Don't leave me."

Buddy was leading the way.

My feet were frozen. They felt like stubs at the bottom of my legs - a means of getting me to safety.

Pain, fear. We were being saved, we would be rescued. I had to follow.

Using a stone to help cut through the cloth, one of our rescuers ripped the sleeves off his sweater and wrapped them over my naked limbs; the frayed threads were comforting on my lacerated feet.

How much farther did we have to go?

Chapter 5

Survival Was Only the Beginning

They were climbing up to bring us down.

They lit a path; there was hope. We trekked across coral and stone. We were being led to safety.

We were survivors.

At the foot of the hill, there was a little car with her engine running. Warmth! We crawled in on top of one another like sardines in a can, but we were safe.

"Inside quickly and close the door, don't let the warmth escape."

Away from the thrusting ship, away from the sinking ogre, away from the towering chimney stack and the freezing Mediterranean. Away from the spiky, splintery, razor-sharp rock and coral and the minced meat it made of my feet.

What remained with us was the cold; the freezing pain of trauma and the destitution and despair of the unknown. The horror of loss, of being abandoned and alone.

Our clothes were wrapped around us like ice packs. But we would be returned home.

I remembered home. We had family who would watch the news and wonder if we escaped. I had to call home.

Windows misted, breathing was heavy, and the feeling of pain and fear dominated. We had no idea of where we were or who these people were that saved us. We had no idea where we were going or how. The moisture was dripping from our bodies and into the seats. Our tears were salty, or was it the salt from the sea?

This little car felt so safe, so solid and warm.

We sat as close as possible, huddled and waiting.

How long did we wait? Time still had no meaning to me. All that mattered was that we survived.

We were guided out of the car and onto a large bus. There were many of us. Laurence and I were no longer alone; we were no longer in charge. These people cared and would help and guide us. We relinquished control and trusted in our rescuers. We felt safe.

There was water on the bus, bottled, clean, crystal clear… the clarity and safety of drinking water.

Gulp, gulp, gulp. Pass it on. So thirsty. Once we cared about drinking from a used bottle. Now it provided a drop of water, a drop of hope, a means of hydration and we passed the bottle on. No one hesitated. Together with other survivors, we became one. We shared all we had.

The engine was running, the heat fans blowing. People outside the bus were making plans we could not understand. We were safely tucked in a cocoon of survival. Where did this lead? Where were we going?

The door opened. A driver took his seat. We were driven into the darkness and away from this scene of devastation.

We didn't care where we were going. It did not matter. We did not have to think. I was exhausted, my energy gone. Thoughts of keeping warm were draining what little energy we had left. We surrendered ourselves into the hands of these strangers as if in a trance.

It seemed an eternity before the bus came to a stop. Shivering and shaking, teeth chattering and body aching, feet burning, so stiff, so cold, I forced myself up. Get up! You must walk, you can do it!

We walked up a dark and steep cobbled path then climbed some stairs. Finally, we were led into an unknown haven, a place of kindness and care. I remember walking through the door into a room down the hallway to the right. This building looked like a small school. There were a few classrooms filled with tables and chairs with children's drawings on the walls. Possibly only three or four rooms, an administration office and two washrooms, two toilets in each. I recall walking into the first room and all I could focus on, was the bar heater along the wall.

We were survivors and these were our care givers. They did what they knew best and gave of themselves freely. This was only the beginning.

"Laurence, I must take off my clothes."

I was wrapped in a white mattress cover, quilted and dry. I could feel my circulation tingling through my joints, battered, bruised and lame as they were. Get closer to the heater…

I must call home.

"Who can understand me? I need a phone. PLEASE HELP ME. I must call our children."

They must hear us speak. They must know that we have survived. They must not hear the news before we call home. The doors of the school house opened as more people arrived. Although we didn't understand, they were speaking a language of hope.

More people, wet and forlorn, a cacophony of tears and pain…

Our hosts tried to call on their cell phones. We could not think. What was the number? What were the international codes? Where was my family? What were we going to say? What time was it? Where were we? What day was it?

We survived!

2:00 a.m. Saturday, January 14, 2012

They dialed, we spoke.

"This is Mom, we have sad news. The ship has crashed, it is sinking. We have been rescued, Dad and I are both fine."

Where are we, who are these people?

"We are on The Island of Giglio, Carlo Pisacane School. Please contact the Canadian Embassy; we need help."

They were bringing in blankets, clothes, and more people.

New cries, water dripping.

These people were bringing in warmth.

There was a young man sitting in a chair speaking to his Mom in a language I did not understand. She nodded while he took off his dry sweatshirt. He was dry. With an outstretched arm, he handed it to me.

My stomach turned when I smelled the stale cigarette smoke, but I could not refuse it. I put it on and it felt so warm.

Another person carrying a hamper of used and outgrown clothes. More people with another bag. I put on pants. The zipper did not work, but these pants felt so good, so comforting and toasty, covering my shivering nakedness. They were old cords; the cotton fabric was crackly and dry.

Laurence also found clothes. He traded with a ballet dancer; she was more comfortable in his leggings and he in her sweats.

Together with other survivors, we laughed and cried, we traded clothes and shared our tales. Mostly all the people were dry; they had been brought across on rescue boats. Many members of the crew came in but they were mostly whisked away. Where were they taken to?

"Buddy, where are you? I want to meet you?" I wanted to hug and thank Buddy and to see his kind and gentle smiling face.

There was a drone of voices and tears. Many conversations in languages we could not understand. We assumed that plans were being made, questions were being asked. We were not being told.

Together we spoke of hope. There was security and trust, and dependency on these strangers. We believed they would work it out as we put our lives in their hands.

The doors opened revealing a huge pot. It was filled with sweet, warm tea. It smelled so good; the sugar regenerated energy and strength, blood tingling, circulation flowing.

Again and again the doors opened, ushering in more people, another load – people in, people out, phones ringing, people sobbing.

A lady walked in and I heard keys jingling and closet doors opening - first aid supplies. They were doing everything they could, and more.

She came over to me with a gentle and smiling face.

"Il mio nome è Valeria Bellau...." I could smell disinfectant. I could feel warm water, a plastic basin, and gentle hands.

The pain, the warmth, the comfort and compassion.

"How do you say fuck, in Italian?" I said, digging my nails into the hands of the people on either side of me.

The pain was electric; it transmitted through my body.

She was holding my foot, one by one, gently maneuvering her tweezers; one more razor sharp sliver out, another piercing shiver. The fear of coral poisoning was magnifying. I must be brave; she will get them all out.

It felt like hours later, the noise around me returned. My feet had been soaked and cleaned. Someone placed soft, dry socks on my lacerated stumps. My feet hurt, but my heart was warming. We survived. We were saved, and were now in the caring hands of unselfishness being offered by total strangers. This was the language of love and of compassion.

I told Laurence that we are so fortunate that we are Canadians. I know we will be amongst the first nationality of passengers and crew to be whisked away and delivered safely back home.

There was a call for us on the cell phone that I had used to call home.

A lady called from the Canadian Embassy in Rome. Franca was her name. She said they were doing everything possible. They were searching for all 12 Canadians reported to have been on the *Costa Concordia.* They know we are safe and would call back when they had a plan.

"I have been told that we need to take a ferry to get back to the main land," I cried to Franca. "I will not go back on the sea, you must send a helicopter for me," I managed to say between my tears. Franca reassured me that we would be safe and they would do whatever was possible to take care of us.

We had made new friends. Together, we laughed and cried. Together we celebrated life.

We would get back to our families. We would get home.

"Vino, vino, vino," I put my hands together and spoke one of the few Italian words that I knew we would all understand.

Within moments, we all spoke the same language, that of unity and affection, of hospitality and humanity, the language of hope and gratitude.

Again, creaking and squeaking, the doors opened and in walked another face, another stranger, another token of good intention, carrying a box laden with bottles of wine.

We cheered. We sipped, "to life, to life, l'chaim, salute." This was our Celebration of Life.

From this moment, I knew these friendships would be sealed.

How much longer would we be here?

Pastries were brought in - a labor of love; they had been baking through the night. More people brought cookies, apples, coffee, blankets, sanitary supplies, diapers, medication and even shoes.

Photographs on phones of missing people were being circulated. Matches were made, bad news was shared, joy and celebration of news of loved ones in other rescue centers, on this tiny Isola del Giglio.

The doors opened, the doors closed. Conversations filled the stillness of the air, the silence of pain, the smells of confusion and fear.

Across the hallway, I noticed the elderly lady we took under our wing on the deck of the faltering ship. She was coming in from the cold. She was safe. We had protected her as long as we could. She must have been brought across in a lifeboat as I noticed she was dry. We had made a justifiable decision as we abandoned her when we leaped into the frigid sea. She had been helped across. We had to let go at the time. We could not have taken her into the sea with us.

For hours she cried. She had been separated from her husband and did not know his fate.

In the early hours of the morning we noticed somebody talking to her. A match had been made; her husband was safe in a Church at the Porto del Giglio.

I noticed her face as she received the news. Her wrinkles were rosy and plump, she became serene and so pretty! She had such soft and gentle hands. She smiled.

Laurence and I looked at each other with tears running down our faces, as we realized that we had done the best that we could have, at the time. I walked across and hugged this beautiful elderly lady, as I thought that she too might be a mother and grandmother. We could not understand each other, but shared this news with relief.

Down the hallway was another classroom. It was dark. Bodies were lying over the tables and across the floor. We could hear the cacophony of snores, the whimpering of tears, the silence of despair.

Across the door was the administration office. Once it facilitated a small island school; this night it was the skeleton, the backbone and spine. From here, the nerves regenerated the courage for all to call home, send faxes, stand in line, work out calling codes, international exchanges and dial numbers.

"Is the internet working? Was there any news on the web," we asked?

"This is me…Mom, Dad, who is this….." What time and day is it? So many other countries, places other people called home?

"Have you heard the news…?"

Some slept, some cried. We shared stories, we compared courage. We were enveloped in a comfort capsule. How long was this going to remain sealed?

The rooms were warm and the hearts intense.

The night was long, we could not sleep. Thoughts of the horror, racing through my head like a nightmare.

Sobs and sighs, chattering of people's recall. Everybody had a story to tell; not everybody was able to share it.

"Take my email address, stay in contact." We were sealing the bond of lifelong relationships.

Could we get home? It was Saturday. Our flight was scheduled on Monday from Barcelona.

We were the Survivors.

MY FIRST FACEBOOK POSTING:

 Andrea Davis January 13, 2012 - 7.37 pm Mountain Time:

Ship Wreck Costa Concordia - WE ARE FINE. Rescue on Island Giglio - Carlo Pisacane School. People amazing, warm, food and safe. PLEASE DONT WORRY - will try to update.

January 30, 2012

Dear Mrs. Valeria, Teachers, Parents, Students and all on the Isle of Giglio:

My husband Laurence and I are proud survivors of the tragic accident of the Costa Concordia on January 13, 2012.

I have attached a few photographs and hope to have you recognize us as you read through this note and share our gratitude to all on this beautiful Island of Giglio.

All our lives, as firstly South Africans and then Canadians, we have read, learned, and dreamed of visiting the Tuscan Coast. Did we ever realize that our visit would end in such trauma and tragedy?

What a truly beautiful island you have; once filled with unspoiled beauty, now shattered with the tragedy, devastation, and debris of the Costa Concordia.

As long as we live, we will truly be grateful to your community for the unconditional rescue efforts, care and compassion that were extended to ourselves, our fellow passengers and the crew of the Costa Concordia on the devastating night of January 13 /14, 2012.

We will never forget the warmth and empathy that unfolded from each and every 'Islander' that came to the school to help out in every way possible during the early hours of that morning. The kindness and compassion was insurmountable, the effort and undertaking was unyielding.

Laurence and I would like to extend our gratitude and thanks to every one of you, in whatever way you participated towards our eventual trip to the mainland which got us one step closer to home and our eventual reunion with our children, grandchildren, family, and friends.

Please remember to thank the people who walked us over the hills, down to the cars, the bus drivers, the 'nurse' who did such an amazing job removing the coral and debris from my feet with such a gentle and caring hand. The tea maker, the suppliers of clothes, shoes and blankets, the people with cell phones. The teachers and children who shared their school rooms with us, who allowed us the use of their computers and the Internet to make contact with our beloved families and to start our calls for help to our homeland Embassies. Even the gentleman who appeared with a bottle of 'vino' within minutes of receiving the call for help.

I now dream of returning to your Island one day. I know I will come one step closer to healing after I have reached out to hug and thank each and every one of you for your unconditional involvement in making a difference in our survival.

We thank you from the bottom of our hearts.

May you be blessed with the courage and support that it will take to one day look back to the sea and remember the sea and nature for their beauty and tranquility, and be able forget these moments, days, and years of pain and suffering caused by this unforgivable disaster.

We wish you beauty and joy.

With love and thanks to all.

Laurence and Andrea Davis

As daylight broke, the doors of the school opened. Wrapped in blankets, we were escorted out and down the stairs along the cobbled path.

The caregivers and comforters hugged and waved to us …. goodbye, "arrivederci e buona fortuna"- until we meet again. The kindness of these angels has created a special place in my heart. This memory will remain embedded in my soul forever.

There were buses lined up. One by one, one step at a time, we piled in, no idea where we were going. Plans were being made for us, people in work-wear came in to give instruction. Italian was spoken. They did not communicate with us. They did not tell us what had happened through the night of Friday 13th. What went wrong or why?

The engine drone started and the door sealed shut. Down the winding road we left Giglio Castello behind. Down another hairpin bend, the ocean was in full view ahead.

My head was thumping, my heart skipped, blood was racing through every artery, tingling inch by inch. She was lying below in the bay, fallen over on her side, hundreds of meters away from the landmark that we had eventually reached, after swimming our way to safety. Exhausted from the battle, she had given up. The reality of the last 12 hours had left me forlorn. Laurence and I hugged onto each other as we gasped and cried.

We reached the port where we were instructed off the bus.

Bone weary, my aching feet and frazzled soul could hardly carry me. One step at a time.

It was cold; the scene of a disaster zone.

It all seemed familiar. The image was just as we see emergency relief images on TV.

Sirens and ambulances, flashing lights and police vehicles. Beep-bop, beep, make way….stretchers were carrying the wounded and injured people were screaming out aloud. "Help, I need help."

A ferry back to the mainland - we had no choice. Back onto the sea, we were told. There was no other way; there was nobody to discuss this with. Where were we and where are we being taken to now? We had no strength to even question as we lined up. People shoving and pushing trying once again to remain together with their family and partners. I heard people talking of being sea sick, hot and stuffy, dirty from the trauma of the night. This trip across, time after time again, the ferry returned and went back. Like cattle into a shed, we were channeled onto this ferry. How would I feel? Once a calm passenger, now a petrified survivor. Hiding within our blanket cocoon, Laurence and I sneaked into the guard office in the lower level. The heavy door squeaked as we pulled it closed behind us. We did not want to follow the masses, people were starting to smell.

Nauseous and cold, I was too tired. I no longer had energy to fight the invasion of foreign elements and senses. There was a tiny bar heater on the floor in the corner hidden under a little desk. This alcove was merely large enough for us to sit on a stool, alongside each other. "Don't leave me," I said to Laurence, as we drifted off to sleep while this heavy and solid transportation ferry, carried hundreds more stranded, destitute and anxious people, one step closer to their homes and families.

An hour later we were woken with a jolt as the ferry made contact with the edge of the pier. Clank, clatter, crunch, as chains were released to tie the vessel down to firm ground. This noise was grueling. Was it only last night that we were fighting the implications of these same excruciating, immeasurably loud and out of control noises? Again, the sounds of people shouting, giving instruction, and making plans for us that we had no part of.

Red Cross stations were set up along the streets. Military stations lined the way to help with the coordination of this disaster. Wherever we looked, there were cameras and reporters.

Disaster junkies were hovering around in anticipation of this wealth of traumatic editorial news that they were now fighting and scrapping for.

The sound of chaos was looming. Angry, agitated and aggressive was now becoming the norm. Where to, why and when?

Nobody asked us anything. Nobody knew who we were, how we had escaped off the ship, or where we needed to go to. Nobody asked us what language we spoke nor where was home.

Eventually, they started filtering this line of stranded, destitute survivors through the doors of the first aid tent. After I had my injured and aching feet dressed, covered and tended to, we were ordered into another line.

Through one side and out another, the drone of counting began .....

There were sheets and sheets of paper, the piles were accumulating.

Name, cruise number and country of origin?

Next.

Buses lined the streets, ambulances, police cars and emergency vehicles, horns honking and sirens billowing. Echoes of our own thoughts and confusion were drowned out by this white noise.

With military command, again we were ushered into another bus.

Just a short drive away to the next emergency rescue station. This time, a large city school building, concrete and cold. Chaos loomed, angry and agitated people shouting in every room. Hands were in the air, bodies shaking in anger. Insufficient, dirty ablutions, flooded toilets, exhausted, hungry and confused survivors, everywhere.

Leora Hornstein - January 14 at 9:29 a.m.

Feeling grateful and thankful for the fact that my parents are alive and safe after their cruise ship sank. They've lost everything - but their lives. Thanks to everyone for kind thoughts and wishes. We're doing everything we can to get them home quickly. Please keep them in your thoughts.

Andrea Davis - January 14th – 12.16 p.m.

Can't get in contact with Canadian Embassy in Rome. Lady who called is Franca. Can't get through to this number. We are both FINE - Please do not panic. Currently at Porto Santo Stefano (Grosseto) School - Giuseppe Mazzini middle school (rescue center). PLEASE NOTE - Laurence's name on PASSPORT IS SPELLED - LAURANCE NEVILLE & ANDREA SUSAN. We have no documentation, $, passports etc. but will be taken care of when she gets hold of us.

Arriving at this school was the first solid step to finding our tracks and making paths to our ultimate journey home. How incredibly hard it was to sit down in the administration office, thinking I would post a note on Facebook so that people around the world who knew we were on this trip would be able to read of our safety and follow us home.

With the chaos of thousands of other survivors, organizers from Costa, Red Cross, First Aid, and desperate souls in the background, I worked my way towards a computer, hoping to be able to feel in command (as I always do) when I have a keyboard under my fingers.

Google icon – click – everything was in Italian!

Facebook icon – click – everything was in Italian!

Desperate, I stood up and wailed between tears, "Please, is there anybody here who talks English? Can somebody help me on this computer?"

"My name is Erica Shamlin Benedetti."

An angel was guided in our direction. From that moment on, Erica took charge. She was in command of communication and translated from Italian to English. Erica spoke with the Canadian Embassy. She dried our tears, took charge, and did not leave our side until she escorted us to the bus that drove us onto the next leg of our relay.

3: ERICA SHAMLIN BENEDETTI AND ME, OUTSIDE THE TRAIN STATION IN PORTO SANTO STEFANO ON OUR RETURN TO ITALY - JULY 6, 2012

Our cruise was booked to embark and disembark in Barcelona. In their effort to direct and take control, Costa began grouping all survivors by their city of scheduled disembarkation.

"All passengers, scheduled to disembark in Barcelona…"

Where to now? The baton had once again been passed.

Laurence and I fell asleep as we drove South through the hills and valleys on our way to Rome. I remember trying to force myself to stay awake, thinking of how I had yearned to make this road trip through the Italian countryside.

I must stay awake. I wanted to devour this scenery. The hills and the vineyards were dry, my eyelids were wet and heavy; my body was lead.

We must get back to the Tuscan coast, I thought, I dream to see this Italian countryside.

We were on our way to Rome where we would be able to coordinate our passage home.

The bus came to a stop. I forced my eyelids open. Where were we? There were so many people, buses, cameras, and reporters – they were all over.

Making our way off the bus, we were immediately bombarded. My feet hurt but we had to walk on.

I don't want our children to see us looking like this, I thought as the reporters and camera crews came closer. Have they seen the news?

"Do you mind if we ask you a few questions?"

Laurence was talking; I looked ahead and let out a scream.

Ahead of me, making her way through the mob of people, I saw and heard Tata. She was wrapped in a beautiful white blanket.

God sent us an angel, I thought as I went running down the pathway to reunite with our beautiful new friend from the five magnificent days of sailing.

4: Reunion with myself and Tata, Laurence watching over us with our "Hobo Bag" safely on the ground

On Friday before the accident, we had spent the day together in Rome and came back laughing and joyous, celebrating friendship. We were having dinner with Mike and Tata when everything went wrong. Was this only yesterday? It felt like years ago.

On that night of terror, when we left the dining room, Mike and Tata crawled in one direction, we in another. We did not see each other again until now.

We were left wondering where they were and if they had made it off the ship. If so, had they survived, were they alive? Once we were safe in the school, there was too much time to think.

We learned that Tata and Mike had made their way onto a lifeboat and had been transported to the port of Giglio. From the port, they were taken across by ferry, and bused into Rome during the early hours of this morning. The Hilton Rome Airport Hotel was their designated hotel.

Miraculously, they were in bed and asleep before Laurence and I were rescued from the rocks.

Laurence, wearing his donated fake sheepskin jacket and carrying his plastic bag over his shoulder, filled with our only possessions, became the icon that journalists were waiting for. And me, in soiled washed out, threadbare sweatshirt, men's corduroy jeans with a broken zipper, the luxury of mismatched plastic 'hand-me-down' sandals exposing my bloodstained and injured feet.

The beginning of the media frenzy and TV interviews.

What were we going to tell them? After a moment of serene thought and pitiful silence, I looked at Laurence and together we began nervous giggles. We did not realize at the time that we had become an icon of what the media was looking for. The perfect picture of destitute survivors of the sunken *Costa Concordia*.

"Imagine what our children will say when they see what we look like." The thoughts were nerve-racking yet gratifying. They will see that we are uninjured and alive, before we are home.

We were ushered into the hotel and asked after checking in, if we would step back out for another interview. It became evident that the media were not allowed into the hotel, but lined up outside, each one flashing bigger and heavier equipment than the other. The battle was on. Who was going to capture the lead story? Who was going to be the first to win the morbid details the media and the world were waiting to hear? All we wanted to talk about was our gratitude for survival. We needed time to think clearly. Give us space. Give us time.

We wanted to get home.

After lining up at the front desk, we were assigned a room. I fantasized of taking a hot bath and putting on clean clothes.

"Do you have a bathrobe?" I asked.

Could I trouble you too for a toothbrush and toothpaste for both of us?

We needed to get our laundry done. Laurence had carried our 'Hobo Bag', over his shoulders since the Island. Our only belongings were wet, pitiful clothes that we had been wearing through the night of the accident and across the sea, as well as my sodden handbag carrying my drenched camera, eyeglass case and lipstick.

"Would it be possible to get our own clothes laundered?" I dared to ask.

"Mrs. Davis, it might be 36 hours," said the front desk manager. "I'm not sure when we will be able to get them back to you?"

"We hope to be making our way back home by then," I replied.

After a few minutes, he made eye contact with me, signaled to me and followed me up to our room. He took my bag of soiled and wet clothes as he left our room.

"I will see what I can do."

I trusted this kind and gentle man with all we had.

We sat on the edge of the bed and picked up the telephone. After struggling with International long-distance lines, again I spoke to the front desk manager and he had the operator unblock the calling restrictions and opened up International dialing access for us.

The telephone lines were hectic; nobody could get past the International exchange.

Around 4,200 stranded people, each having families to be accountable to. All we needed to share was the news that we have survived, we will be coming home.

We had no regard for time zones, we only knew that we needed to call *now*. Was it day or night? How long had it been? How long would it take until we were able to clear our heads and answer unanswerable questions? There was so much coming back to our minds, so much to talk about.

We began calling home, our children in Canada and South Africa and our family in the USA.

"Did we wake you?"

We let everybody hear that we are alive, let everybody know where this latest leg of the journey had taken us.

"Hilton Rome Airport Hotel," I announced.

"Please call the Canadian Embassy again," I asked in despair. "No, we have not heard from them again. We had no way of letting them contact us, but now we are not going anywhere. Our room # is…."

They needed to hear our voices. Our throats were raw from shock, and over and over again, we were telling our story. It was so hard to talk as shock was setting in. This story was becoming real. We owned it. It belonged to us. It was our story.

Shaking uncontrollably, "Yes it is all true," we repeated.

The world was standing by, counting heads, waiting.

How many people remained unaccounted for?

"Death toll rises to six with 17 still missing," we heard.

How can they come up with these numbers I questioned? Until a short while ago, nobody had asked us our name?

I thought we would have been questioned on arrival, "Are you OK Mrs. Davis? How did you and your husband get off the ship? How did you reach the shore?"

No one representing Costa has yet to ask us these few short questions.

By now, the news was global. The frenzy had magnified and mostly the questions remained unanswered. All we needed to share was that we have survived; we will be coming home.

What happened to the ship?

What had caused the accident?

Why was an emergency evacuation not called?

Where were we at the time of the accident?

Were we told what was happening and what to do?

How did we get across to shore?

Where is our luggage and passports?

Do we have any money?

Were we afraid of dying?

We lay on the bed quietly, trying to answer all the questions and processing all that had happened. We had not had time to think of any of this while it was all happening.

One step at a time.

About an hour later, there was a gentle knock on the door. "Housekeeping, we have your laundry."

I cried, this dear lady cried, and we hugged each other. She showed so much respect for our few meager possessions.

We both soaked in the bathtub. Laurence gently cleaning away the remaining debris from my burning feet, gently separating one toe at a time.

The hot water was comforting on my aching and bruised body, my painful and exhausted new hip.

Shampoo, soap, tooth brush and tooth paste. These were sheer luxuries we will never again take for granted when we check into a hotel room. Usually, we open them, smell them and leave them for the next guest or the trash.

Tonight, the bar of soap was worth more than a nugget of gold to me.

We got dressed into our beautiful laundered, dry and clean clothes. They smelled so good and felt soft and warm on our beaten up bodies.

Our telephone rang, "Hello Mrs. Davis, this is Franca Finamore from the Canadian Embassy."

"How are you and how is Mr. Davis?"

Franca explained and apologized for not getting back to us all day but once she had established, back in the early hours of the morning, that we were both safe and unhurt, she and fellow Canadian Embassy employees spent the entire day searching and accounting for all 12 Canadian citizens. "Thankfully," Franca reported, "you have all been accounted for and are all safe."

"Do you need a Doctor?" Franca asked.

"I can wait until the morning."

She promised to send a Taxi for us, "Be in the lobby at 9.30 a.m."

We had a sudden burst of energy. We had to start working things out.

We realized we had hardly eaten in 24 hours; we must go downstairs and find some food.

The hotel lobby was huge and chaotic. Staff from various agencies were attempting to sort out assistance stations, broken down into countries of nationality. People were still arriving in droves. Confusion and aggression was rife. The challenge of the days ahead seemed daunting.

We were shown where to go, down the hallway they had banquet-sized dining stations. The magnitude of the temporary facilities that the hotel staff mustered was humungous.

There was food and drinks available 24/7. There were buffets stations that were continually being replenished and cleaned, changing from dinner to breakfast to lunch to dinner.

Hot drinks, cold drinks, juices, fruits, pastries, cookies and snacks. As if by feeding us, they would somehow make it all up to us. We were never asked for a signature nor payment for anything in the hotel. We must assume that Costa was taking care of all the hotel expenses.

People were uniting throughout the night - talking and meeting up with fellow travelers from their countries. Groups were forming, as if together people were stronger and more capable of getting things accomplished. Intermittently, there was an outbreak of hysteria, screaming and tears. News was filtering in continually; bodies were being recovered and stories were being told.

The news reports were changing by the minute.

Captain Francesco Schittino has been arrested.

After we had eaten, filled with sheer exhaustion, we were on our way back up to our room when we noticed commotion in the lobby. Crates of clothing had been brought in and people were scavenging for suitable sizes….something to wear, something to call our own. Brand new, clean and unworn sweatpants and sweaters. People were grabbing as if there was no tomorrow.

Once I was upstairs I tried on the sweater but asked Laurence to go down and exchange my size, hoping I would have a choice.

I waited and waited. In all his kindness he had taken a while trying to help a single young lady passenger, find a suitable size for her. She was struggling and Laurence did his best, as he always does, to help people around him.

A while later, he came back up, explaining the scene of despair when the boxes were empty and many survivors still had no clothes to wear.

We moved the bedside table away, slid the two twin beds further down the room, pushed them together and as I was drifting off into a deep sleep, I whispered "Don't leave me, don't leave me."

We fell asleep in each other's arms and awoke a few hours later, still clutching onto all we had.

The memories of where we were, where we had come from and what we were facing, startled us out of this cozy moment of oblivion.

"Laurence, we must get up and go down to the computers before other survivors wake up. We need to check our travel insurance, flights and email communication."

The lobby was still quiet as we were among the early risers. We emailed the children, ate a small breakfast, chatted with fellow survivors, told our story, heard other people's accounts, and helped wherever we could. We met and chatted with fellow Canadians, Laurie and Alan Willits from Ontario. Laurie was in tears when she heard of our trauma. "I feel so guilty," she cried. "We did not realize how easy it was for us when we got onto a lifeboat and sailed off to the port. A part of us felt that we were on an exciting adventure."

"We had not even unpacked when the accident happened." Laurie went on to tell us that they had only boarded the *Costa Concordia* on Friday afternoon. They had been on the ship for only a few hours.

Alan asked us if we had any money or if there was anything that they could do to help us?

As we stood chatting, he took off his belt and opened a hidden pocket. He handed Laurence 40 Euros; together we cried.

Tata came down. As she was the only Norwegian on board she was meeting their representative on her own. Other groups were forming and people were heading into the city. Americans, Chinese, Israelis, Indians, Philippinos, Russians, South Africans, Australians, to name but a few - everybody was searching for help.

A young blond lady came up to Laurence. With a strong accent she thanked him for helping her last night and reached out to him with a powerful hug.

Long before 9:30 a.m. we were approached by a stranger, "Mr. and Mrs. Davis, I am so happy to be here to meet you. My name is Franca from the Canadian Embassy. I decided to come and help all our Canadian survivors get together and to take you over to the Embassy office. As it is Sunday, the office is regularly closed. I have a few taxis waiting outside."

 Leora Hornstein - Sunday January 15th

Latest update from my parents - their passports are in the works and they will thankfully be home tomorrow evening. They have been looked after by the Canadian Consulate, and have a few more very basic supplies - my mom is going to get a pair of shoes for her trip home.... dare to dream. They are physically well, injuries have been checked over by a doctor and slowly they will pick up the pieces of their lives - with lots of love and support from those around them. The bravery and courage that they have demonstrated, as well as their love for each other, will forever be imprinted in my mind. They have had an interview, and will be on CBC's The National tonight at 7pm (MST) for those who want to watch. Again,

thanks for all your wishes - the care and support we have all received serves as a testament to the incredible parents, family, and friends my parents are.

We spent a busy Sunday with Ambassador James Fox and the incredible staff at the Canadian Embassy as detailed in the previous chapter. We had no idea of the mammoth task ahead of us, making our way back home.

Andrea Davis Update from Rome Saturday 15th (it was actually Sunday) - morning 8.00 a.m.

Thanks to all for your amazing support. As hard as it has been for us, we understand and appreciate how hard it is for you all around the world. We both passed out and had at least 4 -5 hours solid sleep. Only when we woke did we take stock of what we have to be grateful for and all we have to take care of. Physically TG, neither of us have anything more than a few bruises, scratches, and a lot to remember and be grateful for.

Current status is an appointment at the Canadian embassy at 9:30 this morning to take care of emergency passports, flights and all the red tape. Don't think it is possible to get home today but hopefully by tomorrow we will get up in the air. Rest assured to all, we are well taken care of here, we are at the Hilton Rome Airport Hotel, food and essential clothing and everything that can possibly be done for us. A fellow Canadian has just given us Euro 40; he had a money belt and a few notes tucked inside. Imagine how rich we feel with 40 Euro.

Love to all, your support is with us all the way.

Andrea Davis Update ROME Sunday 1:00 p.m.

Yes, my previous note was supposed to say Sunday. Don't know what day of the week it is (this was only the beginning).

We are at the Canadian Embassy, have completed Passport documents, and they are currently working with Costa to get us home, hopefully flying out tomorrow morning as soon as our documents are ready.
Yahoo, I have a lady taking me to buy shoes and deodorant! Laurence is currently downstairs being interviewed by CBC and loving his interaction with the press. Watch for updates!

This day was a whirlwind. There was a doctor at the Embassy office waiting for me, and other Canadians with medical issues. Happy to have had a clean bill of health reported. "Watch those feet," I was told, "and look out for possible infection; coral poisoning can be fatal." I was given a prescription and it was explained where I would have to be taken to find an open dispensary.

"Everything in Rome is closed on Sunday. Be sure to have a thorough medical examination on your return to Canada."

We completed all documentation, affidavits, made calls to Canada in order to certify true identification and references. We signed an IOU to pay for our emergency travel documents and passports as well a few hundred dollars to travel home with. "This will have to be paid back on your return to Canada," we were told. We could not think clearly, but signed and signed and signed.

We were asked if I could walk to a photo booth "around the corner, just a few blocks away." My slippered, aching feet. Step by step. One more block, just around another corner, across the road, down the street. Eventually, we had completed everything that we needed to.

Franca spent ages on the phone with Costa and the airlines. "Good news. You are booked out of Rome early tomorrow morning. Let's hope your passports will be completed and delivered to your hotel tonight."

We were so grateful to have been treated so courteously, with so much sensitivity and empathy.

Franca handed us a used backpack and wallet, "This will help keep your things together till you get home." We were building up a personal collection:

sweatpants and a sweatshirt, hotel slippers, toothbrush and toothpaste, a hotel notepad and pen, and strips of paper with contact names, numbers and important information.

Another TV interview on the bench in a city park. "Yes, this will broadcast tonight in Canada and around the world."

We were later driven to the city train station to find an open pharmacy. People in every direction, driving, walking, hands in the air, honking, shouting … it felt like daggers were going through my head and knives through my back. "I will take you to buy shoes to travel home with," Franca announced. Store to store we walked, till my feet could no longer move and my head could no longer think or see anything. Get me out of here, away from all these people, take me away from these crowds. The emotional pain was agonizing. How was I even going to get anything onto my feet? I could no longer bear the roaring around me. The noise of the last days was magnified, the pain was intense, my head was throbbing, my eyes felt as if they were covered in gravel.

Take me away, take me to a quiet space. I can no longer move. I can no longer think nor can I see.

She helped us into a taxi, paid and arranged for the driver to take us back to our hotel, hugged and waved goodbye. Such is the life of an embassy worker, drama after drama. How grateful we were to have had this support when we were so vulnerable.

When last did we eat? When did we drink?

Back at the hotel, we pushed our way through the pathway of reporters. We can't do this again, not right now. Now we need to eat, we need to decompress. I need to be me. "The Me" before Friday the13th, "The Me" of yesteryears.

"We are looking for Mr. and Mrs. Davis," we heard as we walked into the lobby.

"I am Mr. ……..'' I was no longer hearing anything. It felt as though I could not process anything around me. Shock, trauma and sheer exhaustion was overpowering all my senses.

"I am working for the South African Embassy in Rome and you are the last two remaining South Africans that were on the ship. We are so relieved to have found you. We now have all our South Africans accounted for."

While we appreciated their determination to find us, we could not help think of the mistaken records being handed over from Costa. "We are Canadians, but thank you." Together we sat and chatted with other South Africans. They too were so far away from home - their dream vacations came to an end before they were even awakened from jetlag. Shattered and distraught.

Through the lobby, down the hallway. How much further could I walk? We had to get food.

I could no longer swallow, bite by bite, piece by piece. When last did we sleep?

We had to make it through another hour or two.

"Mr. Davis, there is a gentleman looking for you in the lobby."

By 9:30 p.m., Ambassador Fox's driver arrived back at our hotel and handed us our Canadian Passports. Our bright white passports were being delivered. We were a day away from getting home.

Temporary passports, sparkling white covers, "sign at the X." I could hardly lift the pen.

We were so proud, so grateful to be Canadian.

I will never forget the sensation of knowing that tomorrow morning we would board our flight to London. From there we would go home.

Our new friends all wanted to share the events of their day with us, their progress, disappointments and their plans.

The lobby was rowdy; people were losing reserve.

We passed on the 40 Euros to Tata. We were now so rich with what we had from our Embassy.

She had nothing, no money, no ticket, no clothes, no help. She had lost her friend Mike too.

Mike was an American; Tata was from Norway. They were friends, travelling on this cruise together. After the accident, in this state of frenzy and panic, sadly he took care of himself. He had received his USA documents and was out to dinner in his new clothes. He was not going to miss out on a night out in Rome.

People were becoming crazy in this frenzy, behaving in ways one can only attribute to this trauma. Tempers were flaring amongst those who were still confused and waiting for answers and direction. Pain amongst the injured and emotionally devastated, as well as excited and yet emotional goodbyes.

Tata and I held onto each other as we hugged and sobbed.

"Promise to let us know when you are home." As we parted, we made a pact to meet up in the summer.

"We love you and will never forget."

Relationships were bonded and sealed.

I could no longer listen; I needed to sleep.

We headed back to our room, packed up our tiny backpack, prepared our flight papers and travel documentation and drifted off.

The telephone rang. I awoke, startled out of a deep sleep. "Mrs. Davis, hope I did not wake you. This is Radio…., I hope it is a suitable time and you won't mind answering a few questions."

"Did I wake you?"

"You are an International reporter and you have no regard for what we have been through? Look up www.timezone.com, Rome, Italy." and with this I hung up. Battles with reporters were only beginning.

It was 4:45 a.m. on Monday morning. Our flight was only a few hours away. "Let's dress and leave," I said to Laurence. "I cannot wait any longer."

Chapter 6

Today Is the First Day of the Rest of My Life

The pain of walking through the airport and our arrival at the British Airways check-in desk without a piece of luggage, a bag, shoes or a smile was more than I was prepared for. I will never forget the moment the attendant asked me how many pieces of luggage we had to check in.

 Andrea Davis - Monday Jan 16th London 2:30 p.m.

UPDATE:

Yahoo, nearly there....

Very hard and emotional day, but we are homeward bound & feeling great! We have been treated really well on the flight from Rome and have been in the business class lounge all day. Had a manicure and went to buy a hairbrush and flip-flops and Dad, the Hugo Boss wallet he has been dreaming of for years. Feel so good to have a bag of our own to carry over our shoulders and walk on clean new shoes.

THANKS to all for outstanding support. Can't wait to let you know when we are home safe and sound!
Stay tuned........

 Andrea Davis UPDATE Calgary 6:35 p.m.

Calgary International Airport:

"Today is the First Day of the Rest of My Life"

Home safe and sound!

We were greeted at the airport in Calgary at the gate of the plane. "We will take you through customs. Any luggage to clear?"

The reality was clear - people have no understanding.

"We have lost everything," I cried and carried on walking our way to customs.

"Welcome home Mr. and Mrs. Davis, we have been waiting for you and are so happy to have you home," we were greeted by the Customs officer.

"Yes, we are grateful to have this white new passport; it was only issued yesterday."

We proceeded to the automatic glass doors. Ahead of us, the doors slid opened ...... flicker, flash, blinking and shining in every direction. Snap, flash, click, click, click....and the moment we had dreamed of.

The moment of reunion with our family.

"Do you mind if we ask you a few questions?"

How can you describe what it feels like to hold your grandchildren, to hug and touch your children?

Was it only two days ago? The moment when we were hours away, minutes away - seconds away from death.

This moment of being together and home was indescribable.

5: REUNITED WITH OUR CHILDREN AND GRANDCHILDREN

LEFT TO RIGHT: EVAN, ME, LAURENCE WITH CALEB, ANTHONY, LEORA, DAVID AND JARON

6: ME, CARIN, LAURENCE WITH KILEY AND BRADLEY

JOHANNESBURG, SOUTH AFRICA

Chapter 7

"We Couldn't Believe It When We Heard"

September 5, 2012

Excerpt from a letter from my daughter – Leora Hornstein:

"The next few days were a complete whirlwind and blur. Media, friends, phone calls and emails - all very concerned about your welfare as we still continued to go about with our everyday business, yet this event was all-consuming. The most difficult day was the following day, Saturday. I couldn't get any information from the embassy until late that night, at which point all they could tell me was that they were working on getting you what you needed, but they had no information about when you would be coming home and couldn't tell me much - except you were safe. In the middle of the night that night, you called and it was so good to hear you were indeed, OK. We waited for the news about when you were coming home - at that point, we could look forward to seeing you and having you back here safely. It seemed like such a long wait and, of course, we were thrilled beyond words when you were back "in our arms".

Mum and Dad - it's been a really challenging few months. Watching you both, Mum especially, being so traumatized from something was so very difficult to witness, especially from an outsider's point-of-view. Having not been there and not really understanding the totality of what you experienced, made it very difficult to empathize from the outside. Mostly, I wished I could help you more and help you to see that what was lost was physical "stuff", and that you two are so blessed and were still meant to be with us. But I realize too how much you have both suffered, and how difficult this has been for you both. Many times, I just wanted my "Mom" back - my "mom" who went on the cruise, not the "mom" who returned who was grieving and suffering so badly. But that's what life is - things happen that take us on our own journeys - and its events and life's challenges that take us on new paths and lead us in different directions.

I hope that this event, as traumatic as it has been, helps you and us, and everyone around you, to realize that life is precious - it can be taken away from us at any time. It has certainly reminded me that nothing should be taken for granted, and that things change in a second of time. I hope too, that through the grief and struggle you have endured, that you are able to turn this event into a positive life outcome, and lead your new life journey in a different direction - one that will hopefully leave you feeling accomplished and fulfilled.

Love you always, and Daddy of course,

Ya. "

The days following our return were a daze. We were bombarded with people, phone calls, emails, and well wishes. The press and reporters were calling day and night.

"Are you the survivors?"

The headlines didn't help:

Cruise ship 'pandemonium' described by Calgarians

'Everything was going pretty smooth until Friday the 13th'

CBC News Posted: Jan 15, 2012 5:41 PM MT | Last Updated: Jan 16, 2012 5:55 AM MT 41

"Everything was going pretty smooth until Friday the 13th," said Laurence Davis. "We call it unlucky Friday the 13th, but in my case it's lucky Friday the 13th because I'm still alive."

CBC News, Calgary - January 15, 2012

Costa Concordia Survivors return home

CalgaryHeralddotcom Subscribe 810 videos

You Tube - January 17, 2012

January 17, 2012 Updated: January 17, 2012 | 5:59 am A A Adjust Text Size

Calgary couple back home after 'horrific' shipwreck

Metro News - January 17, 2012

Couple home after escaping sinking cruise ship

Toronto Sun - January 17, 2012

7: A HANDOUT AERIAL VIEW TAKEN AND RELEASED ON JAN. 14, 2012 BY ITALIAN GUARDIA DE FINANZA SHOWS THE COSTA CONCORDIA, AFTER THE CRUISE SHIP RAN AGROUND AND KEELED OVER OFF THE ISOLA DEL GIGLIO, ON LATE JANUARY 13. (AFP/GETTY IMAGES)

"Oh my God", I heard Laurence shouting from the kitchen table as he opened and looked at the headlines on the front page of the newspaper. "This is the blonde, from the hotel lobby in Rome."

er

CALGARY HERALD

Woman sought as witness to disaster

Blond, captain seen dining, sharing wine

Nick Squires And Victoria Ward, The Telegraph
Published: Friday, January 20, 2012

Domnica Cemortan is emerging as one of the key witnesses to the chain of events that led to the Costa Concordia disaster.

In the days that followed, reality set in.

The empty closets of our home were echoes of pain and trauma.

Telephones, door bells, and eventually empty silence.

How long would this last?

Appointments, doctors, psychologists, lawyers, insurance claim, family, work, children…

How were we going to make decisions with regard to our claim against Costa? We needed to start replacing our belongings, buying clothes, toiletries, electronics and jewelry. Everything we had with us was loved. Memories cannot be easily replaced.

We received mail with a settlement offer. We also received many curious comments and criticism about turning this around to make millions. What kind of compensation, monetary or otherwise, would buy back our sunken belongings, would take away the pain in my feet, or repress the trauma that we have endured? We had to make immediate decisions. We were forced to trust others as our lives were overtaken with extraordinary activity. We were denied clarity, time, and information - everything it took to make informed decisions. We trusted those around us to help us over these hurdles.

Facebook and email messages continued to pour in:

"Oh my God, we have not spoken in 35 years…."

Calls from afar; the entire world wanted to hear a little piece of what we had overcome.

"I could never have done it….."

"What would I have done, I can't swim…?"

"We salute you for your bravery!!!!"

"Are you the couple we saw on TV?"

"We want to hear it all… can you talk to our group…?"

Dear Andrea and Laurence:

I was just reading Cruise Critic and saw your message to me. We arrived home on Saturday evening and were very glad to see our daughter and grandbaby at the airport. We were fortunate that there was no press at the airport!

How are you doing? I have been thinking about you often. You are amazing and it was a privilege to meet you and spend time with you.

We did our interview with The Fifth Estate last evening and they tell me that you are being flown to Toronto early next week for your interview. It was a new experience for us! I look forward to the airing of the show next Friday! I wonder how much of our interview time will be broadcast. Hope your interview goes well and that it's not too hard on you. I have not been sleeping well but I guess that is understandable. How about you? I can't imagine the degree of post-traumatic stress that you must be feeling!

Let's keep in touch and hope we meet again someday under better circumstances!

Take care and be well!

Love,

Laurie and Alan

8: LAURIE AND ALAN WILLITS – FELLOW CANADIAN SURVIVORS FROM THE COSTA CONCORDIA

Mike Plottel - Jan 29 2012

We are so glad you are both OK and survived your ordeal in relatively good shape. We saw many of your interviews on TV and I watched your Global news appearance yesterday. It sounds like you made a good decision when the water started lapping up on your deck! I have also got to say that as a former vessel commander (in my case, an aircraft) I just can't understand why the ship's captain would put his passengers and crew in danger by deliberately overriding his programmed navigation systems and disregarding his company's operating procedures. You trusted the cruise line to keep you safe and it sounds like many of their safety procedures either weren't effective or weren't followed by the crew."

When would the turning point come in this haze that had become my life? I so desperately wanted to have our life back, as it was. We now had so many extraordinary things to deal with. People were continually bothering us. While they were trying to be supportive, there were many hidden issues in the attention. The energy required to answer everybody left us exhausted. Fear of all these changes, the pressure of the red tape that we had to get through, the uncertainty of a possible law suit and eventual settlement. Were we going to settle for the pitiful compensation package that we were being offered by Costa? This would become final . A settlement would impact any possible future claim.

How could we know what would lie ahead of us as a result of this accident, as well as the possible physical and emotional trauma that could manifest as a result of this disaster?

So much paperwork and so many unanswered questions.

How were we able to deal with everything in this vulnerable frame of mind?

People wanted to hear our story. I was getting tired of speaking but we still had so much to tell.

We had boarded the ship as ordinary people; we got off it changed. We were now extraordinary people.

I wanted to find my way out of this darkness. I needed to do whatever it took to come to terms with this tragedy as well as to understand the reality of this incredible miracle of survival.

We were now living through our own Celebration of Life.

Imagine realizing the privilege of receiving the well-wishers, the cards and letters, emails and Facebook posts, fruit baskets, food platters, baking and treats? Everyone we met shared generously of themselves and their resources. Friends offered us clothing and jewelry. Life was not meant to go this way. These types of sentiments are typically expressed to one's family after the passing of a loved one. It is not usual to receive, read, hear and share these sentiments oneself.

Work associates, clients and colleagues, school friends and play mates, teachers and principal - all reached out to touch our lives. These people we will never forget.

"In the many months that have passed, we have spent a great deal of time with Andy and Laurence, and it is clear that their lives have changed. Their stories of the rescue, the heroism of the people of Giglio, and their entire experience resonates with us as we can't help but put ourselves in their place. What would we have done? How would we have coped? Would WE have survived as they did?

One thing I do know is that the experience of watching your friends go through something like this cannot help but change you as well……it did for us.

We have always felt grateful for our health, our family, our friends, and our good fortune in life, but Andy and Laurence's brush with death has truly given us a deeper and more solid understanding of how fragile life can be. We are infinitely more grateful for each day, and certainly for our treasured friendship with Andy and Laurence!"

Linda Gutman – Friend

Chapter 8

Lost Identity

Hours blended into days.

I had little strength or motivation to think about replacing our lost possessions. So much energy was being exerted on regaining our health, embracing our loved ones, and answering the many unspoken questions.

Sleep, meals, daily activities were tormented. The horror of our experience would not leave me.

The pain of our losses was intolerable.

I was told my strength would return; when would it start?

Where was the key? Would I find the ignition?

On January 18, 2012, I celebrated my birthday. The calendar indicated it was my 54th year. Correction! I was 53 + 1. This was a new beginning; my clock started all over again. I would have to relearn how to live, for this is a new life.

I am now a miraculous being, one of strength, determination and recovery.

On the evening of the disaster, I had a small, evening purse diagonally over my shoulder. It had adhered to my chest when I put on the life jacket. There was nothing else between me and the freezing sea.

So much was going through my mind during those final hours.

At one point I had taken my camera out of my purse to capture the blackness on the outside deck. What was I thinking? How could it withstand the elements? My handbag hugged close to me, carrying my only remaining possessions - my lipstick, my prescription glasses and my camera. It held hundreds of irreplaceable photographs covering our South Africa visit, first moments with our baby granddaughter, possibly last memories with many elderly family members and friends. And so many unforgettable memories of our week in Europe, before that fateful day.

Technology allows us to take so much for granted. Wherever we go we are able to capture unforgettable moments with ease. Cameras in our phones and iPads, tiny digital cameras to "point and shoot" and DSLRs. We place our trust in these gadgets expecting them to keep our memories safe. We thought we had it all covered. But Laurence's camera was left in our cabin on that evening. He wanted his freedom to enjoy the evening through his own eyes and not through the lens of his camera. He knew that I would be snapping away at every exciting moment.

Laurence removed the memory card from my camera once we got to Rome. We cherished it and prayed. Would we be able to recover anything?

Within just a few days after our "swim", my camera began to rust. Caked in salt and debris I told him there was no longer any point in hanging onto it. It seemed as if this was all that had remained for us to take home. Although it was now useless, at the time it felt tangible. It was hard to trash this camera, as it had meant so much to us and represented so many memories.

UPDATE JAN 20 2012

I am so excited to have just realized that all my pictures on my memory card that swam across the sea with me, are clearly downloaded onto my computer. It has taken me until today to have the courage to get my card into my brand new laptop computer.... yet another miracle.

The phenomenon of our survival was becoming reality. How could I measure the pain between the loss of my old brown wooden hairbrush that I had been using for 40 years, and the joy and celebration of these overwhelming miracles?

How are we ever going to balance our losses with our gains? While constantly being reminded of our material losses, we were constantly reminding ourselves of our good fortune.

Day by day, I would reach out for something else that was not there. Would our possessions be rescued from our cabin? Would we ever get anything back?

Our cabin is one of the few that lies above the sea. What state can anything remaining on the ship be in? The rescue team, the harsh weather, brutal winter, blazing summer, the sea breeze. What could possibly remain of anything left behind?

In the months and now years that have followed, we have never had any word from Costa, regarding our possessions. We have had no word regarding anything!

I have my life; I have my love. Other losses we could manage.

~~~~~~~~~~~~~~~

On our first day home I visited the Apple store and demonstrated my determination to reconnect with my lifelines. I replaced my iPhone, iPad, and Apple Notebook.

I remember getting into the car and not knowing where to turn my phone on. My head felt as if it was a marshmallow puff.
~~~~~~~~~~~~~~~

Yes, I could get back to work and start all over again. If only I realized then that it was not about replacing our material things.

The days became darker, nights longer, and life more difficult.

The butcher paid for our chicken, the baker paid for our bread. Our friends and family gave us love and empathy. Gifts were offered to us daily. People did not know what to say; the act of giving spoke thousands of words. The generosity was overwhelming. The compassion was incomprehensible.

Where were these life lessons written? This became a passage of time, as we received expressions of kindness that were never taught. It comes from one's heart, expressions from within.

Strangers commented, "I need to hug you." People needed to touch us as the brilliance of this act of connection became greater than any words could express.

I eventually went to buy shoes.

"I can see that you are having a difficult time deciding on these shoes," said the young sales assistant.

Followed by my tears and explanation of why I was replacing my old black sandals, the lady sitting next to me exclaimed that she had seen the TV interview with my beautiful family on our return.

I chose the pair of shoes that I wanted, and stepped forward to pay.

"The lady ahead of you paid for your shoes," the clerk said.

Gasping in disbelief, I ran out to look for her. She was nowhere to be seen.

Acts of kindness performed silently.

"I don't know if I would have been able to do it. I applaud you," we were told. How do you respond correctly? We were lost for words.

Each day, each conversation, each relationship – all would have to start as new. We were not the same Mom and Dad, we were not the same friends, we were not the same professionals; everywhere, we had become story tellers.

I was constantly coaching myself as I did in the sea, "You can and must do it. You will do it."

Jan 20 2012 - Erica Shamlin Benedetti

Hello Andrea and Laurence....I will never forget the both of you. I wish we could've met under better circumstances, but I believe I stumbled upon you two for a reason. I'm so very happy that you called me, as I have thought of you two very often, especially after you got on the bus! I kept wondering how you made out in Rome.

I'm absolutely relieved that you made it home safe and sound...and are able to be with your family. That's what Laurence said before he jumped, right? I remember him telling me he wanted to get home for the kids! It was a significant day for all us. To me, life is the best thing you both got from it and it brought you closer together. I hope to hear from you soon. Let's keep in touch.

Hugs to you all!! Muah!!!!

January 30th 2012 (Calgary Herald, Letter to the Editor)

My husband Laurence and myself are grateful survivors of the Costa Concordia tragedy.

We want to thank fellow passengers and crew who assisted in this rescue, the incredible community of Giglio, the rescue team, all at the Canadian Embassy in Rome and Ottawa, the staff and rescue efforts of the Hilton Rome Airport Hotel and staff and crew of British Airways.

Most of all, our loving family and friends, without whom we would not have been able to get through this survival and our journey home.

Our sincere gratitude is extended to all for kindness, compassion and care extended to Laurence, myself and our family during this difficult time.

Sadly, we remember those less fortunate than ourselves who have been so critically injured and wish them all strong journey to recovery.

To those families who have lost loved ones, our hearts go out to you through your times of mourning.

God Bless you all.

Every night in my dreams, I see you, I feel you ...
My Heart Will Go On .....

~~~~~~~~~~~~~~~~

Feb 13 2012 (Translation from Italian)

Hello Laurence and Andrea,
I am Valeria, the school's caretaker or how you called me the "nurse". You don't know how much I am relieved to know that you are home warm with your family and friends.

I am truly happy that our nightmare is over also if met each other under horrible circumstances. I remember you both very well and I would be happy to have you visit our wonderful island for a beautiful vacation.

I passed your letter around to all the people that were present that night and I also posted your letter on the door at our school.

It's wonderful to see that you both are safe again!

One month has already passed, but I will remember you always and I can't thank you enough for the memory that you left to me.

I wish you good fortune and joy.

With Affection,

Valeria
~~~~~~~~~~~~~~~~

March 6, 2012

Nearly two months since that grueling night. Not one day of peaceful rest. Not one moment without these memories. Not one second of life as it was. There is only life before and life after. Day by day, we love, we laugh, we cry. We know our destiny is not our choice.

> *"The Chinese use two brush strokes to write the word "crisis". One brush stroke stands for danger, the other for opportunity. In a crisis, be aware of the danger-but recognize the opportunity."*
>
> John F. Kennedy

We booked our tickets, we must go back. We must reunite with and celebrate the gift that we were given: the gift of Life.

Chapter 9

Regaining Trust in the Sea Our Incredible Journey

"I now dream of returning to your Island one day, when I know I will come one step closer to healing, after I have reached out to hug and thank each and every one of you for your unconditional involvement in making a difference in our survival."

I had promised and believed that this was the next step in our "Incredible Journey". Our tickets were booked; we were going back.

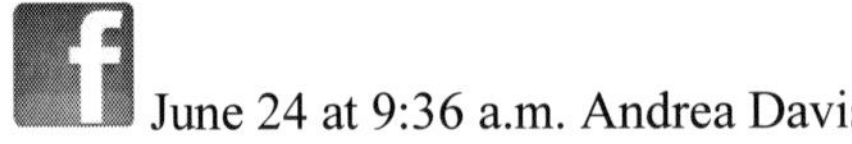

June 24 at 9:36 a.m. Andrea Davis

As we approach six months after our cruise accident, Laurence and I have recently decided to return to Italy where we will retrace our journey of survival as we head to Giglio from Rome. We plan to visit briefly with all the amazing people along the way who were influential in helping us to get home and reunite with our dear family and friends.

This is both very exciting and mostly tumultuous.

We will return home via Amsterdam, from where we will be cruising Paris,

Brussels, and the Norwegian Fjords. Along the way, we will reunite with a dear friend (living in Norway) who we met on the Costa Concordia and were together with at the time of this accident, we were taken separate ways.
Afraid, nervous and excited we will sail away on Friday, July 13.
We are hoping this trip will be both cathartic and a closure, enabling us to move on. Will it give us the confidence to continue cruising and traveling which we so love?

It is inconceivable to think of the significance of these two events both holding so much dependency on one's belief in the superstition that has been instilled in us, regarding *Friday 13th.*

While Friday the 13th is supposedly an ominous date, steeped in superstition and assumed by some to bring bad luck, we now feel more inclined to turn the tables and value the comfort of our belief that Friday the 13th is our lucky day.

My Facebook communications had strengthened our friendships and the excitement over our return to Italy was growing. Messaging had sent out word that we were on our way back, returning along the route of our journey of survival.

But where to begin? I had no idea what distance we had travelled, how much land we had covered, nor how many relationships had been formed, bonded, and sealed between Rome, Porto Santo Stefano, and Giglio.

I needed to return; to drive back over the Tuscan hills to the Port of Santo Stefano, where we had first met Erica Shamlin Benedetti, at the mainland rescue center. Erica helped us get back home; six months later she helped me plan our return. It would be an incredible reunion.

"From the Rome Fiumicino airport, take two trains and a bus, then I will be there to meet you," Erica wrote.

9: ERICA, ANDREA & FABRIZIO BENEDETTI, ERIANNA, AND ALIZE

Anticipation over the next few days was unimaginable. Would we recognize these people? How were we going to feel? We could not imagine what this trip would uncover.

I was so excited. I was so sad. The complexity of these emotions was overwhelming. Above all of the chaos and confusion, I was so grateful that we were blessed with the opportunity to return and express our gratitude to our rescuers.

10: The port at Porto Santo Stefano

Porto Santo Stefano is a quaint Italian port and village. This was our initiation to our journey and our reintroduction to the path we had traveled in pain and trauma. When we arrived on the morning of January 14, 2012, we were just two of hundreds of traumatized, exhausted, and ill survivors being brought here by ferry.

This had been the first identity checkpoint. The Military regiments had organized us into Red Cross help stations.

"Name? Country of origin? Next!"

What number were we? How many missing? How many dead?

11: PICTURE TAKEN BY ALAN WILLITS WHEN THEY ARRIVED AT PORTO SANTO STEFANO

Today we were survivors. We were back to relish the glory of our victory. We had overcome and were back in high spirits, with loud voices and a huge presence. We needed to make ourselves heard; we needed to say thank you, to touch the stepping stones and become acquainted with the beautiful souls who had forever taken residence in our memory.

We cherished the miracle of survival. We were beginning to understand the role that each memory would awaken as we retraced this inconceivable passage of time.

How could we have envisaged the Port in this glory if we had not traveled back? We had a privilege and opportunity to erase the horror of the past and replace those memories with the beautiful reality.

12: BEAUTY AND TRANQUILITY OF THE PORT AT PORTO SANTO STEFANO ON OUR RETURN

Our next step was the ferry back to Giglio.

"Call when you are leaving," we were told via Facebook, "and we will be there to meet the ferry."

Our approach towards the Island was marred. The memory of Holocaust education came rolling back to me as we approached the wreck. We were facing the sight of a cold, callous, rusty, sunken, and pathetic heap – a memorial to our trauma and the loss of so many innocent lives. The rock jutting out of the wreck was a dagger to our hearts. I was overcome with horror, the memories of mutilation and destruction ignited.

The miracle of our endurance.

Surviving the wreck was only the beginning.

Determination brought us home, persistence and tenacity our driving force.

When we left the ship we felt so big, the wreck so small.

Now, standing here, the wreck was so big and we, so small.

At the time we had felt so brave and so proud to have won the battle with this vessel. In the months that followed, this trauma has grown in huge proportions, leaving us to feel so vulnerable and at her mercy.

We survived.

13. OUR APPROACH TO GIGLIO ON THE FERRY AS WE GET OUR FIRST VIEW OF THE TRAGIC REMAINS THE SHIP WRECK

14: THE COSTA CONCORDIA SHIP WRECK. JULY 7, 2012

The miracle of our healing was reaching this point of realization: we had been given the choice. Who was the driving force, the generator of courage?

We were victims; were we now heroes?

We had chosen to live.

We would walk along the path, touch the rocks, swim the sea, and reach out to the sunken thief that attempted to steal our lives.

Arms wide open, we would embrace the miracle of our destiny.

"Your return to Giglio to say thank you, is truly a testament to your character(s). It's a moving example of TikunOlum (a Hebrew phrase that means "repairing the world"). This situation was a completely avoidable disaster that has taken its toll on everyone involved. Yet less than a year later, you and Laurence have been able to keep the anger in check, choosing instead to focus on the

positives - saying thanks to your rescuers, appreciating your new and ever lasting relationships with the people of Giglio, and enjoying the beauty of Tuscany. What I take from this is how fortunate I am to have you in my life."

Notes from a friend – Gail Steinberg

"What a brilliant, brave and very positive thing to be doing! I am sure you and Laurence will have a most wonderful time with many special moments with the people you met. I am excited for you."

A note from our cousin – Simon Fish

Silently, the ferry docked along the port of Giglio.

The vision was etched in our memories. The pain was still raw.

We looked up and saw the welcome of waving hands, the extension of hearts of joy. We were welcomed back onto the Island of Giglio as if we were returning home.

15: VALERIA BELLAU AND LELA (EMANUELA) BANCALÀ, WELCOMING US OFF THE FERRY - JULY 7, 2012

Not speaking a word in a common language but sharing expressions of love and gratitude, we were immediately driven away. We were taken up to the closest view point and stood in awe. The wreck still lay along the rocky shoreline to which we had swum, climbed, and trekked to reach our point of discovery.

16: VIEW OF THE SHIP TAKEN FROM THE ROCKS THAT WE CLIMBED ACROSS

Our reunion was jubilant. As quickly as the locals gathered to help us that evening, so quickly they gathered again on this afternoon. The expression of love and gratitude was overwhelming. We had united in desperation but reunited in a spirit of hope and love.

The afternoon proved to be an outstanding victory celebration aimed to banish the shadows of the recent calamity.

17: WELCOMING HANDS OF FRIENDSHIP, SNACK BAR, IL PORTICO GIGLIO CASTELLO

18: THE PHOTOGRAPH OF THE SHIP WAS TAKEN BY GIUSEPPE MODESTI, PRESENTED TO LAURENCE ON ARRIVAL AT GIGLIO CASTELLO

LEFT TO RIGHT: STEFANIA PINI, ANDREA STEFANINI, GIUSEPPE MODESTI, VALERIA BELLAU AND GINA BARTOLETTI, EMILIO BANCALÀ, TERESA CRISTINA BANCALÀ TOGETHER WITH LAURENCE

Our days on the island were a whirlwind of love, laugher, and encouragement. We met everyone involved and heard about the events of that night. We laughed, we cried, and we listened to stories of their parts in our rescue and the plight of 4,200 other passengers from the sunken *Concordia.*

"I took this photograph at 11:40 p.m. and then watched the ship sinking."

"I saw the beacons flashing off your life jackets and notified the police there were people stranded on the rocks."

"I climbed up the rocks to show you the way down, lighting up a walkway with only the light of my cell phone."

"I opened the school, to bring you into a shelter of warmth and safety."

"My mom sent in a huge pot with hot tea, smothered with sugar. We hoped this would revive your energy."

"I brought you pants."

"My husband brought you Vino."

"After baking through the night, we brought in croissants in the early hours of the morning."

We were told tales of the events following the evening, days and months thereafter.

We met with Deputy Mayor Mario Pellegrin, Chief of Police Roberto Galli, and many more dignitaries. We were told of the miraculous nature of our escape. The exact time the ship went down, of our courageous maneuvering over the vacuum and turbulence created by the sinking vessel. We heard about those who had disappeared. Was it hypothermia? There were so many unanswered questions. We heard of those trapped and injured. We talked about the rescue efforts on the ship and on land. We spoke of the cowards, and the glory of the heroes. We spoke about the destruction to the reef and heard of the void in tourism. We heard about the plight of the Islanders, the impact on their lives, and the strain on their livelihood. Behind their smiling faces we read their pain.

Between the lines we heard laughter and song; we saw happiness and warm hearts.

We rejoiced and celebrated together. We ate, laughed, and drank.

We bathed in the sun on the beautiful warm beaches and swam in the gentle tranquility of the Mediterranean.

We gathered together to share, and mostly to express our gratitude.

"As we stand before you all on this beautiful Island of Giglio, I refer back to my earliest communication to you all, shortly after our return to Canada.

As long as we live, we will truly be grateful to your community for the unconditional rescue efforts, care and compassion that were extended to ourselves, our fellow passengers and the crew of the Costa Concordia on the devastating night of January 13 /14, 2012.

We will never forget the warmth and empathy that unfolded from each and every Islander that came to the school to help out in every way possible during the early hours of that morning. The kindness and compassion was insurmountable, the effort and undertaking was unyielding.

Laurence and I would like to extend our gratitude and thanks to every one of you, in whatever way you participated towards our eventual trip to the mainland which got us one step closer to home and our eventual reunion with our children, grandchildren, family, and friends.

It was my dream to return to Giglio. A mere six months later, we stood on the very rock that was our first stepping stone on solid ground; it led to our survival.

The pain before our eyes is unforgiving, the sorrow in our hearts inescapable. But each day forward brings more gratitude and love, and less devastation and fury. We are determined to survive.

"The one thing grander than the sea is the sky. The one thing grander than the sky is the spirit of the human being." – Anonymous

"Without you all, we could not have done this. We thank you from the bottom of our hearts.

You will always be courageously remembered."

19: Our presentation of the symbolic Inukshuk*
to the people of Giglio

Left to right: Deputy Mayor Mario Pellegrini, Laurence Davis, Mayor Sergio Ortelli, Andrea Davis, and Chief of Police Roberto Galli

*INUKSHUK is an Inuit word meaning "image of man's spirit". Originally, the Inuit built these manlike sculptures of rock along Canada's northern shores as markers to lead their way. Today they serve as symbols to remind us of our dependence on one another and the importance of strong relationships!

We were taken back to the school house and shown the rooms, the heaters, computer, and the phones. On the wall were the letters I had written, the letters of thanks from us and other survivors. We had left our mark, now a permanent feature.

We were escorted through their village, their homes, the school, the cafes, over to the beaches, the pebbles and the sand. Savouring the tranquility of gratitude, we enjoyed the true beauty of Italy, basking in the sun on the soft beaches of Campese, eating Gelato and drinking wine. This was the way Italy was meant to be experienced.

20: BEAUTIFUL BEACHES OF GIGLIO, CAMPESE BEACH

21. SUNSET TAKEN FROM GIGLIO, CAMPESE BEACH

22: OUR TOAST "TO LIFE"

After five magnificent days, we were driven down the hills and back to the port. We boarded the ferry and continued on our journey of healing and love.

We left Giglio, remembering love and laughter, happiness and tranquility. We were moving on to our next stepping stone; one step closer to healing.

On our return from this trip, once I had decided to write this book and capture the expressions of so many people, in communication with Val I asked her to share 'just a few words'. What I value most is her expression of *Friendship*.

 Aug 28, 2012

Hello Andrea,

will be difficult to re-live that night but I shall gladly do hope that it serves to share the great gift that both you and Laurence you left me .... Our FRIENDSHIP!

a hug

VALERIA

P.S: I'll do it as soon as possible!

23. THE ORIGINAL DRAWING OF 'THANKS' DONE BY THE SCHOOL CHILDREN

24: THE ADMINISTRATION OFFICE AND COMPUTERS WE USED

Dear Andrea and Lawrence
How are you?
We are the students of the school of Giglio island. We know what happened the last Jenuary and we hope you are good now.
We are writing you to tank for the present you gave us.
We really like the Inukshuk statue and its symbol.
We decided to expost the gift, so that every one can appreciate it
We celebrate the tragic anniversary whit a mess. It was very emotional.
We know you are writing a book about what happened that night on the Concordia.
We hope you'll come soon to visit our island, it would be a pleasure to meet you.
This is a picture of all of us.
We are proud of our little school.
Big hug from our island.

P.S.: would you like to be our penfriends? We would you like to write you again.

25: THIS LETTER TOGETHER WITH THE PHOTOGRAPH WAS RECEIVED ON MARCH 15, 2013

Living life with our family still whole is really all that matters in the end when I think about the ordeal. The accident can be looked at as a tragic event for my in-laws, or an opportunity to set a different course on their future years as to how they choose to live their lives.

David Hornstein – son-in-law

One more stop – back to Rome. It took us an entire day to get there but we were determined to reach the people at the Canadian Embassy. The staff had worked relentlessly, day and night, to track us down, manage our safety, and take care of our every need while we were destitute and distraught. They did everything possible to be supportive and diplomatic. They reconnected our identity, nurtured our immediate needs, arranged passports, and coordinated arrangements to get us back home.

O Canada! Our home and native land.

Chapter 10

Our Return to the Oceans

Friday July 13, 2012- Six months after the tragic accident of the Costa Concordia we set sail on The Royal Caribbean's *Brilliance of the Seas.* We sailed out of Amsterdam and visited Brussels, Paris, and Norway. We were extremely anxious but very excited. I cried for days leading up to the trip. The anticipation was overwhelming. Every move I made, every step I took, the air that I breathed - our recent nightmare lived with me.

I was reminded of the horror and realized the fear will never leave me.

We had a remarkable trip, filled with apprehension, courage, and excitement.

The trip brought back to mind every moment of our love for the sea, and the wealth we have gained and collected along the way. We have covered thousands of miles since we began cruising in 2007.

We were given a hero's welcome and were treated like royalty. We were welcomed back onto the ocean by the crew of Royal Caribbean and fellow passengers.

We were spoiled with flowers in our Stateroom, gifts of wine, fruit, and bouquets of flowers.

Glasses were raised as we were "toasted" endlessly by new friends and fellow cruisers. Everybody wanted to hear our story; everybody wanted to share in our plight.

"We could never have done it," we were told repeatedly.

26: We toast as we sail out of Amsterdam

27: A memorable day in Paris

28: THE INDESCRIBABLE BEAUTY OF NORWAY

29. We Cherish new friends: Joan and Sheenagh Walker – Ireland

30: Bob and Carol Peterson – USA

Before sailing, we were instructed to report to deck four and Muster Station eight. Together with all passengers, we were educated in emergency drills.

This will remain an unforgettable experience. So many thoughts were provoked, goose-bumps standing up like soldiers across every inch of my body. As I looked out at the sea, memories came rushing back at me.

We chose to do this - together we wanted to return to the open waters, to renew and reinstate our love of cruising. I held on to Laurence. We looked at each other; we cried together, and then we smiled.

The culmination of this journey was our reunion with our dear friend Tahereh Hojat in Stavanger, Norway.

When we left Rome on January 15, each returning home in our bamboozled state, we promised to visit in the summer. Laurence and I selected this itinerary, knowing that we would be able keep this promise. We are so grateful to have been able to make this happen.

On day three of this cruise we spent the most memorable day together with Tata, a time of healing and gratitude. Together we laughed and wept tears of happiness and joy. Mostly we celebrated the privilege and gift that we had been granted - the gift of Life.

31. ANDREA AND LAURENCE DAVIS WITH TAHEREH STAVANGER, NORWAY

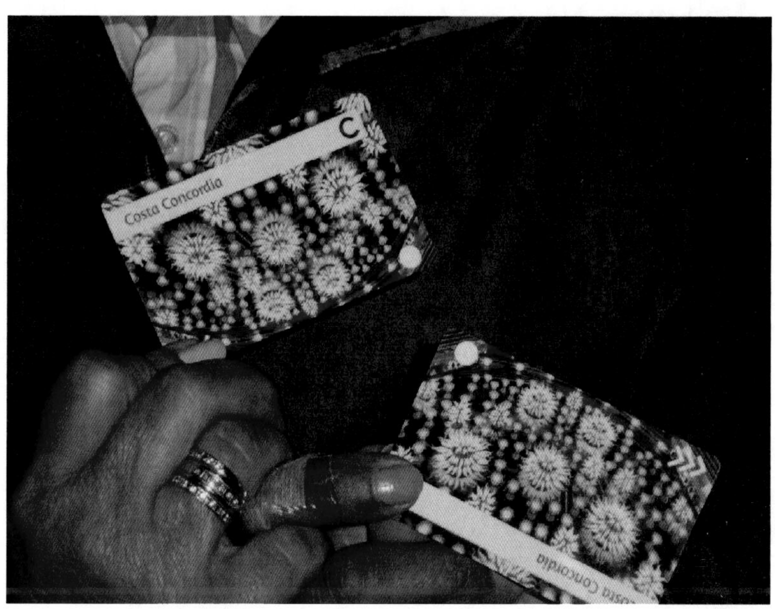

32: Laurence and Tahereh both saved their CostaConcordia Identity Cards

33: We find an Apple Store in Stavanger to share this recent Internet post of our reunion in Rome on Saturday January 14, 2012

In the months that have passed, we continue to sort through an array of emotions.

Inspiration and gratitude transition between times of disturbance and despondency.

Yet I notice an evolution.

We become cognizant of the reality of having lived through and survived this horror.

I do not feel sorry for myself. On the contrary, I feel grateful to be alive.

I feel proud and honored to be called a "Survivor".

We are stronger; we are richer in all of life's values.

Recovering from the physical and mental trauma of these punishing blows has presented formidable challenges. We realize our vulnerability daily. We understand the needs of our family and friends have changed through this life-altering experience. We are reminded that people have a need to reassure themselves of our presence and our well-being. We will never be the same two people who set out on a beautiful Mediterranean cruise on Friday January 13, 2012.

I had a profound revelation: I have a choice to be a victim or to go forward in the light of these challenges.

Laurence and I would like to thank all who stood by us during these months, for encouraging us to believe in ourselves and our purpose for survival.

"When everyone around you says you can't.
When everything you know says you can't.
When everything within you says you can't.
Dig deeper within yourself, and you can find that you can."

Mark Elliot Sacks

Chapter 11

Talk to me about PTSD

"And a woman spoke, saying, Tell us of Pain.
And he said:
Your pain is the breaking of the shell that enclosed your understanding."

The Prophet – Kahlil Gibran

Post Traumatic Stress Disorder is an anxiety disorder characterized by reliving a psychologically traumatic situation, long after any physical danger involved has passed. - Canadian Mental Health Association.

Days turn into weeks, weeks into months and now - a year. At times this pain intensifies, my understanding of this described syndrome of PTSD becomes more vivid and personal.

We hear and read about soldiers returning from war, people living through an accident or an explosion, people suffering the trauma of physical assault or torture.

And now I hear myself and others speak of surviving the sinking of the *Costa Concordia* and mourning the loss of 32 people that we did not even know.

Since immediately after our rescue, it has been evident to me that people who know and care for me are looking to recognize symptoms in my behavior in order to address me with a new label, as if this is supposed to happen to me. There was no waiting for this to start, no time given for these symptoms to become evident.

I remember being told immediately after the accident, "consult with your Doctor as soon as you return home." I was left waiting for symptoms to manifest, anticipating, imagining. What must I expect?

One year later, I am still waiting, not to recognize the symptoms but now, I await this "illness" to leave me.

Evidently, without any control, it became obvious that I have been susceptible to this condition.

I never knew much about Post Traumatic Stress Disorder. People spoke to me of this in a whisper. Is this happening to me?

I never believed I would succumb to this label or diagnosis. I have always been the one to cope in troublesome times. I have always been the one to be called the caregiver, the pillar of strength or the solution to other people's problems. I am the one who copes in extraordinary circumstances, the one who could always be called a sincere and true friend, a friend to turn to in times of need. I am also a person who questions the science of psychology and wonders about the motivations and the truth of helping people who are confused. It is all so mysterious.

What I think I know about all of this has simply come from watching movies and reading books. This does not happen to people I know, nor to people like me.

On the recommendation and referral from my Family Doctor, I began consulting with a psychologist soon after our return home.

I was struggling to understand PTSD but the reality for me has been that there were months that I spent crying and in tears. There have been times of feeling totally overwhelmed and that I do not want my family to see how upset I am most of the time. They don't know me like this and I choose not to want to talk much about it. I realize my relationships with those near and dear have suffered. Their patience has been extraordinary and supportive yet assertive in their guidance towards my healing. Many days I shoulder emptiness and lethargy while I carry this front of continuing to be the entrepreneur, manage and strive to grow my creative one-person business. The wife, the homemaker, the Mom and best Grandy, as my grandchildren relate to me in merged pronunciation of "Granny Andy".

The giant marshmallow that fills the space in my head on days when I feel like nothing other than a puffy, fluffy blob in a hollow space, yet other days this same space is so busy and so full. It feels as if my head is overpowered by a tangle of worms. They speak to me of sleepless nights, of reliving the trauma, nightmares and terror.

I drive around, forgetting where I am supposed to be going, on a road that I have driven down for 15 years. I forget which way to turn. I miss appointments that have been scheduled in my day planner. Meetings that I had been looking forward to, I forget to attend. I challenge and battle my feelings of listlessness for exercise as my swimming regimen becomes progressively more difficult to maintain.

I question the complexity and reality of all this happening around me. Can this really be the person that I call *me*?

I remember when my world was a safe place, when the days were predictable and when I believed that horrible things don't happen to good people.

I have had sessions of EMDR and in discussion was told "it works for most people" but there is no guarantee. Eye Movement Desensitization and Reprocessing incorporates elements of cognitive-behavioral therapy with eye movements. Treatment is thought to work by "unfreezing" the brain's information processing system, which is interrupted in times of extreme stress.

Hypnosis therapy and counseling are other methods of treatment and yet for me the therapy that I know and trust most, will be self-help and time. Time will help me to move on, time will allow me to get back to the person I used to be, the lifestyle we used to live as well as for these memories to fade into the distant past.

Disassociation kept me safe and got me off the ship. Now disassociation has outlived its usefulness.

I will work through this until the reality of survival overpowers the vulnerability of this awful disorder.

I realized the value of my relationship with my wonderful psychologist was no longer working for me and that I was struggling to see the light in our relationship when I openly admitted to her at a recent visit, "friends have become my psychologist and my psychologist has become my friend". My visits became less frequent, imagining and willing these symptoms to one day disappear.

I will regain my senses and ability to control. I will recognize when I am in a state of resistance and relearn to embrace the situation. I will also allow myself to embrace and to connect genuinely in the trust of friends and loved ones. I will anchor out of this disassociation and back into my body, becoming healthy, using my senses and absorbing the information I am given.

I will look forward to tomorrow and enjoy the people and fragments of life that I love so much. The small and simple things that at times, I feel denied and so out of control. It will all come back to me. Love of life will be appreciated, natural and complete in its entirety.

Again I will plan vacations with enthusiasm, and enjoy every waking moment with anticipation, intensity and joy. I will read a book and watch a movie with Laurence and enjoy this luxury that I once took for granted. I will never again take for granted my enthusiasm for life and my gift of memory. The moments when ones memory is a blur, the thoughts of yesterday is sometimes confusing.

These are the fragments that I have recently been denied, the slices out of a cake or the wedges out of a pizza that disturb the perfection and completeness of being.

The beauty of sleep will be restful and filled with tranquil dreams.

I will welcome this day, as the following day of the rest of my life.

Although it is evident that there is no Band-Aid and no time limit, periods of strength alternate with periods of weakness and vulnerability.

Day by day, I have more clarity and cope with more and more.

Chapter 12

From Rocks to Riches

January 16, 2012

"Your courage, bravery and strength are an inspiration to us all.
We know that God was looking after you and we thank
Him for bringing you back home."
Riva Shein, friend – Edmonton

We have been asked so many times if this experience has brought us closer to each other, closer to God, and if our relationships in general have changed.

I sincerely believe that we had Divine guidance during the hours of this disaster. When I think about and have to answer questions on how we coped and how we felt during the hours on the ship, the swim to land, and the time spent on the rocks, this period felt like eternity. I have no recollection of how long each period was, or what motivated us to move on at each crossroad.

I do know that I was protected. I think back on my emotions at the time and all I can think of and identify with was a warm glow of peace. I had been transported into a capsule of survival, comforted by an aura of calm and serenity. I had been handed a divine gift: the strength to overcome. Around me I saw commotion and chaos. Within me there was determination and tranquility.

How can we answer these questions truthfully and know what it took to get us through those tumultuous hours? All I know is that we did live through the pandemonium, surrounded by chaos and confusion.

Together, Laurence and I were faced with making the choice between life and death.

Was this in our hands? Was each move discretional? Or can we say in a state of self-reliance that we had turned the ultimate over? We relinquished ourselves to faith and trust.

We made the choice when we got off the sinking ship, we reached the rocks, we climbed up the cliff and now we have been endowed with this invaluable wealth and richness.

Our history has become the pillar of our lives.

We must believe.

Epilogue

Will we ever be able to forgive and who are we blaming?

"I fucked up," Francesco Schettino has been quoted from transcripts taken from the evidence of the Black Box. He was in command on the ship at the time of the accident.

He has been accused of causing a shipwreck, abandoning ship before all passengers debarked, and 32 counts of manslaughter.

The lighter side is the humor of the constant reports of how Schettino "accidently fell into a lifeboat" and happened to have been wrapped in a warm blanket when he got across to safety at an area close to port.

Timeline of Events per The Fifth Estate – CBC News

FRIDAY, JANUARY 13

5:45 p.m. Alan and Laurie Willits of Wingham, Ontario, board the ship in Civitavecchia, a major seaport about 80 km northwest of Rome.

7:45 p.m. Angelo and Danielle Pezzino reach the 11th deck Club Concordia restaurant for an 8 p.m. reservation.

8:30 p.m. The Pezzinos, the ship Captain Francesco Schettino and his blonde dinner date enter the restaurant and take a window seat.

9:05 p.m. Captain Schettino is seen in the Concordia Club with Domnica Cemortan, an off-duty ship hostess and translator, and another officer. A witness says the group had consumed at least a decanter of red wine, although Schettino says he drank no alcohol that night.

9:08 p.m. Francesca Tievoli, whose brother Antonelli Tievoli is the ship's chief steward, posts on Facebook: "In a little while the Costa Concordia will sail so close so close."

9:30 p.m. Angelo Pezzino sees an officer walk over to Captain Schettino's table and whisper something to him. A few minutes later the officer, the captain, and his dinner date leave the restaurant.

Approximately 9:40 p.m. Captain Schettino allegedly calls Tievoli to the bridge saying: "Antonello, come see, we are very close to your Giglio." Witnesses claim Tievoli, standing on the bridge, tells Schettino: "Careful, we are extremely close to the shore."

9:42 p.m. Captain Schettino is at the helm of the Concordia when he steers the ship into rocks off the island of Giglio while trying to perform an "inchino" or sail-past salute for a former Costa Cruises captain and chief steward Tievoli.

Domnica Cemortan is also on the bridge when the accident happens.

Alan and Laurie Willits, who are watching a magic show in the theatre, are forced out of their seats when the ship suddenly tilts toward the port side. The lights go out and people start leaving the theatre.

9:45 p.m. The ship is listing by seven degrees and some passengers begin to realize that something is wrong and phone relatives. One passenger calls his parents in Tuscany, who call the local Carabinieri, who then calls the coastguard in Livorno on the Tuscan coast.

10:05 p.m. Captain Schettino calls his employers, Costa Crociere, to report a problem with the ship.

10:06 p.m. Police in Prato contact the Harbour Master's office in Livorno. They say a woman has called to say her mother is on the Concordia, that the dining room ceiling has fallen on her and that the crew has ordered passengers to put on life jackets.

10:14 p.m. The Harbour Master contacts the Concordia asking if it is having problems. An officer replies that it's only a blackout which has been going on for 20 minutes and which they will fix shortly. The Harbour Master asks about passengers putting on life jackets, but the officer insists it's only a power outage.

10:16 p.m. Guardia di Finanza (finance police) patrol boat G104 is close to the island of Giglio and asks if it should check the Concordia.

10:17 p.m. The Harbour Master informs superiors there may be more wrong with the Concordia than the ship's officer is letting on.

10:26 p.m. Forty-four minutes after the Concordia's collision, the Harbour Master contacts Captain Schettino. Schettino says the ship is taking on water through an opening on its left side and the ship is listing. He says there are no dead or injured. The Harbour Master asks if he needs help. Schettino requests a tug boat.

10:30 p.m. The ship is listing by 20 degrees.

Mario Pellegrini, deputy mayor of Giglio, arrives at the port after receiving a phone call from the police telling him there was a ship sinking there. He decides to board the ship to help with the rescue effort.

10:34 p.m. Fifty-two minutes after the collision, the Harbour Master contacts the Concordia, which sends a "distress" message. They are now evacuating the 3,208 passengers and 1,023 crew members from the ship.

10:39 p.m. A Guardia di Finanza patrol boat reports the ship is leaning heavily to one side.

10:44 p.m. One hour after the collision, the Guardia di Finanza reports the Concordia is grounded.

10:45 p.m. Captain Schettino denies the ship is grounded, saying it is floating and that he will try to bring her around.

10:48 p.m. The Harbour Master asks the Concordia to consider abandoning ship. Answer: 'we are considering it'.

10:58 p.m. Twenty minutes after issuing a "Mayday" signal and one hour and 16 minutes after the collision, Captain Schettino tells the Harbour Master he has given the order to abandon ship.

Shortly after 11 p.m. Deputy Mayor Pellegrini climbs aboard the ship using a rope ladder and finds pandemonium as passengers and crew rush the lifeboats.

11:23 p.m. The Concordia reports it has a large tear on its right side.

11:37 p.m. Captain Schettino says there are still 300 people on board.

Approximately 11:58 p.m. Witnesses see Captain Schettino wrapped in a blanket getting on a lifeboat.

SATURDAY, JANUARY 14

00:10 a.m. Local authorities say there is not enough room for all evacuees on Giglio and that they will begin to transfer them to the mainland.

One hour and 12 minutes after the evacuation order, Laurence and Andrea Davis cannot get into a lifeboat and decide to jump in the water and swim to shore. Laurence's wristwatch stops when it gets wet.

00:12 a.m. The Guardia di Finanza report that lifeboats can't be launched on the left side of the ship.

00:34 a.m. Captain Schettino says he is in a lifeboat and can see three people in the water.

00:36 a.m. The Guardia di Finanza can still see 70 to 80 people on board including children and the elderly.

Approximately 00:30 a.m. Angelo and Danielle Pezzino reach shore.

00:38 a.m. A rescue crew in a helicopter sees many people on board and some in the water.

00:42 a.m. Captain Schettino and all his officers are in a lifeboat. Captain De Falco, who is in charge of the Harbour Master's office, orders them to get back on board to coordinate the evacuation.

00:50 a.m. The Harbour Master's office takes control of the rescue operation.

1.04 a.m. A helicopter lowers an air force officer on board who reports 100 people are still waiting to be rescued.

1:45 a.m. An officer confirms that a rope ladder strung across the hull is safe to use.

1:46 a.m. For a second time Captain De Falco orders Captain Schettino to get back on board using the rope ladder.

2:00 a.m. Laurence and Andrea Davis reach the local Giglio island school which is being used as the rescue shelter.

2:29 a.m. Three people are reported hanging from the prow of the ship.

2:53 a.m. A Guardia di Finanza officer boards the ship using a rope ladder and says that Captain Schettino has been seen heading towards port in a lifeboat.

3:17 a.m. Carabinieri identify Captain Schettino on the quay at the port on Isola Del Giglio without detaining him.

3:44 a.m. An air force officer on board reports there are 40 to 50 people left to evacuate from the ship.

4:22 a.m. The number of passengers remaining on board falls to 30.

4:46 a.m. Six hours after the collision, the ship's evacuation is complete.

5:00 a.m. Captain Schettino calls his 80-year-old mother Rosa, telling her: "Mamma, there's been a tragedy. But don't worry; I tried to save the passengers. I won't be able to phone you for a while. Just stay calm."

34: Gashes in the hull of the Costa Concordia, off the west coast of Italy, on January 14, 2012

(Reuters/Stringer)

35: Firefighters on a dinghy examine a large rock emerging from the side of the luxury cruise ship Costa Concordia, the day after it ran aground

(AP Photo/Andrea Sinibaldi, LaPresse)

36: ITALIAN COAST GUARD PERSONNEL PASS ON THE BLACK BOX OF THE WRECKED CRUISE SHIP COSTA CONCORDIA. JANUARY 14, 2012

(AP PHOTO/GREGORIO BORGIA)

37: COSTA CONCORDIA CRUISE LINER CAPTAIN FRANCESCO SCHETTINO (RIGHT) IS ESCORTED BY A CARABINIERI IN GROSSETO, ITALY, ON JANUARY 14, 2012. SCHETTINO, THE CAPTAIN OF THE ITALIAN CRUISE LINER THAT RAN AGROUND OFF ITALY'S WEST COAST, WAS ARRESTED ON THE CHARGES OF MULTIPLE MANSLAUGHTER, CAUSING A SHIPWRECK AND ABANDONING SHIP

(REUTERS/ENZO RUSSO/ANSA)

I question the reaction of the Costa Crociere, its safety procedures, evacuation command and senior officers, officers, and crew members in command. I question the equipment on the ship and the navigation tools that led the ship to the rocks. I question the lack of crisis management and emergency response.

Over the months that have followed, I cannot help but endorse what was largely missed in the media frenzy that developed after the accident. The genuine examples of strength and compassion displayed by so many members of the crew must be shared as a testimony to bravery and determination.

"Buddy," I thank you for leading the way; for your guidance and strength on the path to safety across the top of the rocks. You will remain in my heart forever.

"Lorenzo," I will never forget the image of you on the ferry, the morning of January 14. We had been taken across from the rescue center at the school. You had just arrived at port having spent the night on the sinking vessel doing everything humanly possible to help. As a senior officer, after more than 12 hours of trauma, you exemplified a hero and gentleman. Your bravery will never be forgotten.

You shared with us the evidence of your lacerated hands, bleeding and stripped of skin from tugging on rope, fighting gravity, and helping people to safety, throughout the night. Sheer exhaustion was evident in every word you said while describing your plight of courage and determination. Your narrative spoke of a grueling night helping fellow crew and passengers escape from their potential coffin; lifting them through elevator shafts, pulling bodies up from sunken cavities.

You stood upright in your uniform with pride, the epaulettes on your jacket lying broadly across your shoulders. Your shiny gold buttons and insignia, although ripped and tattered, still sparkled in the bright morning sunlight. Your once white jacket was now streaked with blood and grease.

Yet the pride you portrayed will remain embedded in my memory.

You greeted us, you smiled, you hugged and commended us.

We salute you.

We will not let the traumatic memories destroy our love of cruising. We have been given a gift: the blessing of survival.

Furthermore, we have been granted the ability to forgive the cruise industry and to return to and embrace the sea. We take comfort in our trust of our own destiny.

We encourage everyone to have confidence in the seas and to cherish and nurture the beauty and joy that is derived as a passenger on one of the thousands of cruise ships sailing across the open waters of the oceans, seas, rivers, and fjords.

It is such a privilege to be able to meet so many incredible people, to travel to remarkable destinations, to learn about and see magnificent cultures. Likewise, we are so grateful to be able to soak up the comfort, the majesty, and the glory of being a pampered passenger on a cruise ship.

As part of this fraternity we will never be alone. We have made and cherish new and old friends and look forward to meeting new people along the way.

"How many cruises have you been on?"

"What number is this for you?"

Common questions on every journey.

Proudly, we now answer "Seven and a-half." So many more to go.

"I don't know if I would have been able to do it," we are told on a regular basis.

We will not give up on this, either in self-pity nor in fear, and will encourage every person who is second guessing themselves or the cruise-ship industry, to realize that this was a unique and once in a lifetime catastrophe. We encourage you to believe in our confidence.

To those thirty-two people who ended their lives on this unforgiving night, we commend you for your fight and the courage it took to get as far as you did before being laid to rest.

We will never forget.

And so we begin!

If not for the *Costa Concordia*, we would not have known the joy and warmth of standing alongside the lighthouse at the Port of Giglio holding onto each other so dearly, thanking one another for the strength and compassion that we shared, thus enabling us to turn this into the miracle of our survival.

If not for the *Costa Concordia*, we would not have known the feeling of gratitude that came from sitting along the dock and capturing the spirit of our return to Giglio with my paintbrush and art pad in hand. I was able to live a lifelong dream of painting whilst in Italy, along the Tuscan coast.

LIGHTHOUSE

PAINTED BY ANDREA DAVIS
THE PORT OF GIGLIO, JULY 9, 2012